Clinical Implications of Personality for Mental Health Practice

Clinical Implications of Personality for Mental Health Practice explores the importance of personality traits that shape all forms of psychopathology seen by mental health clinicians.

Patients in mental health settings can have problematic personality traits or a diagnosable mental disorder or personality disorder, many of which do not respond to standard treatment. The author argues that taking personality profiles into account is essential to understanding why people have variations in emotion, cognition, and behavior. The chapters review a wide range of research on personality within a broad biopsychosocial context, including interactions between genetics, neural networks, positive and negative life experiences, and resilience. The book shows how personality profiles (using the Five Factor Model) are important for understanding a wide range of mental health conditions, and reviews the biopsychosocial model, applying its theory to personality development. It argues that certain personality traits can raise the risk of mental and personality disorders, examines how these conditions can be diagnosed, and discusses practical applications of personality theory to clinical work. Case vignettes illustrate how therapists can apply an evaluation of personality trait profiles to individualize treatment and help their patients, and—to a certain extent—modify personality.

This book is essential for psychiatrists, clinical psychologists, and social workers, as well as students in these fields.

Joel Paris is Emeritus Professor of Psychiatry and a former department chair at McGill University in Montreal, Canada. His main research interest is borderline personality disorder, and he is the author of over 200 peer-reviewed articles, over 50 book chapters, and more than 20 books.

Clinical Implications of Personality for Mental Health Practice

Joel Paris

Routledge
Taylor & Francis Group

NEW YORK AND LONDON

Designed cover image: Kubkoo © Getty Images

First published 2026
by Routledge
605 Third Avenue, New York, NY 10158

and by Routledge
4 Park Square, Milton Park, Abingdon, Oxon, OX14 4RN

Routledge is an imprint of the Taylor & Francis Group, an informa business

© 2026 Joel Paris

The right of Joel Paris to be identified as author of this work has been
asserted in accordance with sections 77 and 78 of the Copyright,
Designs and Patents Act 1988.

All rights reserved. No part of this book may be reprinted or reproduced or utilised
in any form or by any electronic, mechanical, or other means, now known or
hereafter invented, including photocopying and recording, or in any information
storage or retrieval system, without permission in writing from the publishers.

For Product Safety Concerns and Information please contact our EU representative
GPSR@taylorandfrancis.com. Taylor & Francis Verlag GmbH, Kaufingerstraße 24,
80331 München, Germany.

Trademark notice: Product or corporate names may be trademarks or registered
trademarks, and are used only for identification and explanation without
intent to infringe.

ISBN: 978-1-032-85809-8 (hbk)
ISBN: 978-1-032-84384-1 (pbk)
ISBN: 978-1-003-51994-2 (ebk)

DOI: 10.4324/9781003519942

Typeset in Sabon
by Newgen Publishing UK

Contents

Introduction

The Purpose of This Book

I have written this book for mental health clinicians, students, and members of the educated public. It will focus on how individual differences in personality are crucial for understanding variations in emotion, cognition, and behavior. These profiles describe differences among normal people but are also important for understanding psychopathology and the treatment of patients.

The term "personality" has been defined in various ways, but the most succinct goes back many decades to a pioneer in the field (Allport, 1937). It describes individual differences in emotions, patterns of thought, and behaviors that shape the way that people process life events. These are *traits*, that is, characteristics belonging to a person. This means that some people react to stressors in life by having symptoms, while others do not. Personality trait profiles promoting either vulnerability or resilience are the most useful way to account for individual differences.

The origins of personality are complex. Crucially, these traits are shaped by *interactions* between genes and environment. Personality is partly heritable and partly due to life experiences. Individual differences in personality can be observed in early childhood, when they are usually described as *temperament,* but later experiences eventually shape temperament into stable traits (Rutter, 1987, 2006).

The origins of most mental disorders can be illuminated by taking personality into account. These characteristics make some symptoms more likely, and others less likely. This means that the same treatment can work for some patients but not for others, even if they have the same diagnosis, and that responses to therapy can be due, at least in part, to differences in patient trait profiles.

The main theme of this book is that mental health clinicians need to consider personality in addition to symptoms when assessing and treating their patients. Focusing entirely on symptoms as targets for intervention is a tempting but misleading option. Mental health practice need not be based on symptomatic diagnoses alone but should focus on the *transdiagnostic* trait profiles that lie behind distress and disorder.

This book will show that personality traits are crucial for understanding almost all forms of psychopathology, not only personality disorders. It will examine what determines personality development, and how traits influence physical and mental functioning, both in the clinic and in the community.

Surprisingly, some psychologists in the past have doubted that personality exists. Mischel (1968) argued that emotions and behaviors are driven much more by situations than by stable traits. These objections were influential at the time, possibly because in the postwar era, the role of heritability in psychology aroused as much fear as respect. But a history of denial of the reality of personality was part of a wider trend in psychology to emphasize the role of the environment, and to downplay underlying biological processes rooted in genetics and neuroscience.

One would like to believe that such beliefs belong to the past, but that is not so. Psychopathology can still be attributed almost entirely to early life adversities that are labelled as "trauma", without considering the inborn temperamental factors that shape risk and resilience. A contrasting idea, equally narrow-minded but currently popular among medically trained psychiatrists, is that psychological symptoms are almost entirely due to abnormal neural circuitry (Insel and Quirion, 2005). Both views fail to consider that *interactions* between genes and environment are what shape outcomes.

For this reason, this book will recommend the application of a *biopsychosocial* model to personality (Engel, 1980). This theory has been previously used to understand the complex roots of chronic medical illnesses and most mental disorders. In a biopsychosocial context, personality trait profiles cannot be accounted for by single causes but emerge from complex developmental pathways involving interactions between biological, psychological, and social risk and protective factors.

I will discuss a large body of research, mainly based on behavior genetics, showing that personality traits are moderately heritable, with genes accounting for nearly half of the variance in outcome (Jang, 2005; Plomin, 2018). These characteristics appear as individual differences that are present at birth, and that remain fairly stable over the life span (Rutter, 2006). In this way, personality traits develop, at least in part, from differences between individuals in the way the brain is wired.

The other half of the variance affecting personality development is environmental, that is, psychological and social factors. But life experiences alone do not shape personality in a consistent way. Stressful events, particularly during childhood, have measurable effects, but are highly variable between individuals. Their impact on functioning can best be understood in the light of interactions with the traits that process them. Moreover, the environmental factors in personality are "unshared", that is, not strongly influenced by growing up in a particular family (Jang, 2005). That is why, in many ways, siblings can be no more similar in personality than perfect strangers (Harris, 1997). That is also why we need to apply a personality theory based on the roles of both genes and environments.

Unfortunately, mental health clinicians, like most of us, have difficulty in thinking interactively about nonlinear relationships (Schiepek, 2009). Many therapists prefer to believe that single causal factors shape specific forms of psychopathology. What we need is to adopt a balanced model of heredity and environment. On the one hand, reducing all disorders to the effects of genes and neurons can be used to support a belief that most mental disorders can be treated (or cured) with biological interventions alone. On the other hand, psychotherapists can make the mistake of seeing most of the symptoms they treat as due to early life adversities. Both approaches fail to take individual differences in personality into account.

When mental health clinicians see patients, the first thing that impresses them is symptoms. Depressed patients feel hopeless or suicidal, anxious patients are driven by fear, patients with eating disorders are uncomfortable with their bodies, substance users center their lives around access to drugs, and patients with personality disorders do not get along well with other people.

The truth is that we do not know enough about the causes of most mental disorders. That is why the *Diagnostic and Statistical Manual of Mental Disorders* (*DSM-5-TR*; American Psychiatric Association, 2022) and the International Classification of Diseases (ICD-11; World Health Organization, 2018) only describe catalogs of symptoms that cluster into syndromes. We lack the data to support a classification of illnesses disorders rooted in a causal model, in the same way as diagnoses in general medicine. Developing that kind of model depends on a level of progress that belongs to the future.

For now, clinicians need to pay more attention to personality. Behind every symptom is a unique person, who will be susceptible to some life events but not to others, and who will react differently to challenges in the course of development. Many forces drive symptomatic phenomena and the diagnoses based on them. But trait profiles are clinically relevant for understanding and treating almost all patients with psychological symptoms.

Clinicians trained, as I was, in psychodynamic models, were all too long ignorant of the power of genetics. Most of us eventually moved on to use theoretical models rooted in the present, not in the past. We no longer need to resurrect formulations based on early life adversities, or on inferences of unconscious mental processes that cannot be measured. The problem with all such models was that there has never been any way to make them reliable and valid. The point of view of this book will be empirical, applying models rooted in data and strong research support.

In summary, this book will explain how and why personality plays a central role in psychological development. There is now a very large research literature on normal variations in personality, and even more extensive data on mental disorders. Yet with the notable exception of personality disorders, a large gap remains in the relationship between these two domains.

In my own profession of psychiatry, research on mental disorders published in journals is now more likely to be oriented to biology. In contrast, most research published in psychology journals continues to be oriented to the effects of the environment. Studies from one side of this divide will not always be read by clinicians on the other side. We need to build bridges between these domains, using an interactive model that helps us understand how personality shapes both normal variations and psychopathology.

The Relevance of Personality to Clinical Practice

Clinicians benefit from applying personality to their work with patients. Unfortunately, the study of trait profiles has fallen victim to popular misconceptions leading to a number of myths about what it is and is not. Donnellan and Lucas (2021) offer a list describing many of these false claims—that situations are more important than traits, that personality is not a predictor of life outcomes, that there is a single gene for each trait, that evolutionary perspectives are not relevant, that there are entirely discrete personality types, and that personality measures can be easily faked. They also consider as myths the use of less valid tools in assessment, such as projective tests or unstructured interviews. It is a myth that traits lack consistency across the life span, or that personality is entirely stable after age 30. It is a myth that traumatic life events shapes personality disorders, and that parenting practices are the main source of personality differences. It is a myth that personality is radically different across cultures, and that men and women have dramatically different personalities. Finally, it is a myth that clinicians cannot successfully treat personality disorders.

All these misconceptions will be examined in this book, and I will review research showing that none of them are based on evidence. But while personality traits are partly innate, and affect functioning throughout the life span, they can be usefully modified in psychotherapy. Clinicians should not be hesitant to apply what I have called *working with traits* (Paris, 1998). Personality profiles are important enough to be robust predictors of mental and physical health. Since traits account for differences in the way people process life experiences, they need to be targeted in psychotherapy.

This book will review various methods of personality assessment, but it will focus on the Five Factor model (FFM), the system that is best supported by research (Widiger, 2015). The five factors are extraversion, neuroticism, agreeableness, conscientiousness, and openness to experience. These domains have relationships, either as risk or protective factors, with a wide range of mental symptoms and disorders (Bucher et al, 2019). But as we will see, the most important factor in psychopathology is *neuroticism*, the tendency for emotions to be intense and unstable.

Why is personality not already central to mental health practice? The answer lies in the relative simplicity of observing symptoms and targeting them in clinical interventions. Moreover, biases arise when psychologists use standard methods designed to manage anxiety and depression. Many therapists today depend on a toolbox rooted in cognitive behavioral therapy (CBT) methods for every symptom. But since classical CBT does not specifically address the modification of trait profiles, we also need to teach patients skills in emotion regulation, curbing impulsivity, and managing close relationships.

This book will argue that changes in cognition, emotions, and behavior, even small ones, can go a long way to modifying personality traits that leads to better functioning.

The Structure of This Book

Chapter 1 will begin by defining what we mean by *personality* and how we can measure it. Describing traits that shape individual differences in behavior, cognition, and emotions is not simple. But personality profiles are relatively stable and do not change radically over time. Although we have no biomarkers related to traits, a large body of psychological science has shown that they can be reliably measured. This is usually done by self-report and/or clinical interviews. Most researchers prefer to use well-designed questionnaires, based on factor analyses that identify the domains on which individuals vary.

While many systems have been developed to classify personality traits, the FFM (Widiger, 2015) is the most researched and has been the subject of thousands of research papers. The FFM describes variations in personality traits in community populations and is equally useful for classifying psychopathology. It is not an accident that the FFM is similar to models developed to classify personality disorders that have been introduced in models such as the ICD-11 (World Health Organization, 2018), and the Alternative Model for Personality Disorders (AMPD; Widiger and McCabe, 2020), currently listed in Section III of the DSM-5-TR (American Psychiatric Association, 2022). Thus, personality traits can be measured as *dimensions* that describe both normal and abnormal profiles. Doing so allows them to be assessed quantitatively rather than qualitatively.

Chapter 2 will show how personality has a broad and powerful impact on our lives: how healthy we are, how long we live, how successful we are in work, and how stable are our relationships. It will examine the strong relationship between personality and both physical and mental disorders. In relation to physical health, trait profiles can, at least in part, shape the risk for illness and the chances for longevity. There is a tradition in medicine, now less influential, that relates specific diseases to specific personality patterns. But a better way of thinking about these relationships is that they are final common pathways are partly governed by genetic variations. The best view of these processes is that dysfunctional traits promote problematic lifestyles.

Chapter 3 will summarize a large literature concerning different methods of personality assessment and will review their advantages and limitations. It will explain why some of the most prominent methods of assessment from the past are rarely used today. While normal assessments of personality are most frequently used in research, they also offer added value to clinical evaluations, identifying problem areas above and beyond symptoms and that can be targeted in treatment.

Busy clinicians need to make rapid personality assessments. With that in mind, this chapter will suggest that we can obtain a useful approximation of trait profiles that are clinically relevant, using a combination of detailed interviews and standard questionnaires. This is why I will recommend the use of inventories (in their brief versions) that have been developed to measure the FFM or similar models.

Chapter 4 will focus on the biological factors in personality. A large literature shows that personality traits are moderately heritable. Research in behavior genetics has found that at least 40% of the variance in traits can be accounted for by heritable factors. The mechanism of genetic transmission involves variations in the formation of neural networks that shape development. Some of these variants are rooted in embryonic development, but mature brains continue to develop during childhood and adolescence and is only complete around the age of 25. This process involves migration of neurons into patterns linked by the trillions of synapses in the adult brain. Biological processes under genetic influence drive the building of these neural networks, but there are also random factors in building a "connectome"—not surprising in view of the complexity of brain development (Mitchell, 2018).

I will also show how the development of personality affects the life course. Temperamental variations are present at birth but are somewhat unstable until they are further shaped by environmental factors. After childhood, temperament remains largely stable over time. Thus, for most people, and for most of the time, personality works well and does not require major changes.

Yet personality-based problems afflict many of those who develop diagnosable psychopathology. Individuals most at risk are characterized in the FFM by high neuroticism, as well as low levels of agreeableness and conscientiousness. These profiles are risk factors that lead to serious difficulties in managing a social environment, particularly when life adversities amplify traits that are already problematic. This is less true for more severe disorders (such as psychoses) that are less rooted in personality. But in common mental disorders (anxiety and depression), temperament plays a crucial role in shaping vulnerability. Finally, a positive personality profile is the main basis of resilience to adverse life events in the course of development.

Chapter 5 will review the role of life experiences, both in childhood and adulthood, on trait profiles. It will emphasize how personality shapes the way we react to life events, both positive and negative. Trait profiles can "bend the twig" of personality, but adverse events do not, *by themselves*, determine whether traits lead to clinical disorders. Instead, personality profiles set boundaries in the extent to which good or bad events modify or intensify traits.

Personality helps us to understand why most children exposed to traumatic or neglectful environments do not develop mental disorders as adults. That is what is meant by *resilience* to adversity. Resilience is not exceptional but is highly ubiquitous. It is by far the most usual response to trauma and other negative life events. That is why we should assume that people who suffer from mental disorders as adults have necessarily experienced a traumatic childhood.

Again, the most correct model is that the effects of life experience on psychopathology are processed through personality traits and are best understood in terms of gene-environment interactions. These interactions have also been described as *"differential sensitivity to the environment"* (Belsky and Pluess, 2009). Some personality traits make some people easily derailed by adversity, while others protect them from developing psychological symptoms. A failure to understand these relationships may lead clinicians to overvalue the effects of adversity and/or traumatic experiences, both early and late in development. Downplaying heritable traits has led to a bias favoring interventions that focus on the past, but that can be less effective if they do not consider these differences in sensitivity.

This chapter will also show that, even if they are not always recognized in clinical work, social risk factors also play a role in personality development. The first and most consistent social predictor of mental disorders is low socioeconomic class, which tends to undermine resilience. A second is "social defeat", related to racial discrimination, which has been shown to raise the risk for some psychoses. A third derives from the radical individualism of modern society, which can be problematic for many people. A fourth is social contagion, which is particularly important for adolescents influenced by peer groups. Specific forms of psychopathology show marked increases in prevalence when one or more of these factors come into play.

Chapter 6 will aim to put the various pieces of risk and resilience together within a single biopsychosocial (BPS) model, using this framework as a guide for adopting a broader and more evidence-based view of psychopathology and its treatment. This chapter will counter the critiques from some quarters that sees the BPS as vague or nonspecific. A biopsychosocial model leads to a flexibility that avoids attributing the cause of mental disorders to any single variable. Our minds tend to be more comfortable with single causes and direct pathways to outcomes. Yet the world of human personality is interactive and complex at every stage of development.

I will review the present scientific status of the BPS model and apply its theory to personality development. I will show how the BPS helps to explain the wide gap between risk factors and outcome emerging from research. I will also argue that future studies of the etiology of mental disorders need to consider multiple factors, and to carry out studies that consider both biological and psychosocial risks. Moreover, in view of the "replication crisis" that afflicts research. It is also important to have a large enough sample to analyze data with multivariate statistical methods.

Chapter 7 will apply these principles to some of the most common symptomatic presentations of mental disorders in clinical practice. However, the disorders that arise from these symptoms are more complex than they seem, reflected in the fact that a significant number of patients do not respond to standard treatments. That discrepancy can be accounted for in part by personality traits that interfere with learning more functional patterns of behavior and emotion regulation.

These principles will be illustrated by showing how personality traits raise the risk for both the most common and most severe forms of mental disorders. Pathways to psychopathology depend on gene–environment interactions, in which traits lead to vulnerability, but also to vicious cycles in which traits are further amplified by maladaptive behaviors and emotions, leading to even further distress.

Chapter 8 will focus on the relationship between personality traits and personality disorders (PDs). Disorders develop when traits become amplified to a clinically significant level. But PDs tend to have massive "comorbidities" with other diagnoses, mainly because pathological traits affect a wide range of behavioral and mental processes. In most of these patients, we see high neuroticism, low agreeableness, and low conscientiousness. These traits may be present in childhood, but often become clinically apparent in adolescence, and go on to seriously affect development in adulthood. I will then discuss how PDs are diagnosed in several different current diagnostic systems, particularly *DSM-5*-TR and ICD-11. It will also show how both these models are compatible with the FFM.

Most of the research on PDs has focused on borderline personality disorder (BPD), a condition that can be highly disabling and that carries a risk of death by suicide. I will discuss how these patients, who are mostly female, tend to be misdiagnosed. I will apply the theory of dialectical behavior therapy (DBT; Linehan, 1993) in which BPD is understood in an interactive biopsychosocial model. BPD is common, particularly when structured interviews are used to identify it in patients. BPD can often be diagnosed in outpatients, and are even more common among inpatients. While many PDs get better with time, they can leave a residue of dysfunction related to underlying trait vulnerabilities.

Chapter 9 will examine the role of personality differences in providing psychotherapy, and how they can guide the strategy and tactics of treatment. I will also show how psychological treatment can, to some extent, modify personality. Since helping patients to use their personality traits in more functional ways can make—or unmake—the goals of therapy, understanding personality traits can lead to a more evidence-based practice. This chapter will then discuss some of the more practical applications of personality theory to clinical work, again based on clinical applications of the FFM.

Chapter 10 addresses problems with access to evidence-based psychotherapies, which are less than adequate.

This book concludes with a brief epilogue summarizing its conclusions and recommending some directions for further research.

Chapter 1

What Is Personality?

Defining Personality Traits

Science studies human beings in two ways. The first consists of *universals* that apply to everyone. The second is a range of *individual differences* between people. *Personality* describes individual differences, that is, the ways in which people differ from each other in how they think, feel, and behave (Allport, 1937). The *APA* dictionary (American Psychological Association, 2015) states that this construct refers to enduring characteristics and behavior that comprise a unique adjustment to life, including traits, interests, drives, values, self-concept, abilities, and emotional patterns.

This description is complex, but so is personality. Let us unpack the crucial word *enduring*. Personality has no meaning if it changes greatly over time and circumstance. Research has supported the view that while personality evolves to some extent over the life course, its core characteristics remain stable (McCrea and Costa, 2013).

Any good theory of personality needs to be supported by research. This chapter will not depend on clinical impressions, but on what empirical data tells us about trait profiles. Notably, variations in personality are not only limited to humans, but also are present in animals of all species (Ogden, 2012). These profiles have been shaped by natural selection to deal with environments that change over time. Each is a *trade-off* that works most of the time, but that also has down sides (Nettle, 2009).

The idea that people have notable individual differences in the way they think, feel, and behave can be traced back to the Greeks (Horwitz, 2021). But many early attempts to develop theories were derived from armchair speculations that have not survived attempts at empirical validation. In the past century, that was the case for theories based on psychoanalysis (Fisher and Greenberg, 1977; Paris, 2022). Today, experts on personality speculate less and base their theories on empirical data.

Research on personality has generated thousands of articles in peer-reviewed journals over several decades. Several journals are entirely

DOI: 10.4324/9781003519942-1

devoted to this domain. Research findings show that while people must respond to specific situations, the *processing* of life experiences is shaped by differences in trait profiles. Thus, similar experiences affect different people differently. These variations do not necessarily describe extremes on a spectrum, but alternative ways of coping that can be normal or abnormal.

It is important to distinguish personality from PDs. Under the influence of currently popular paradigms, personality has become part of common parlance—especially in describing people we don't like. For example, calling someone "narcissistic" may only mean that a person is perceived as difficult and selfish. But by itself, being difficult does not meet criteria for a disorder. Some of the most creative people in human history would have fit that description. The plus side of narcissism is ambition.

So why do personality traits differ so much between individuals? And why do all people not have the same personality? Evolutionary psychology has developed a powerful theory to answer these questions (Buss, 2024). This model hypothesizes that personality variations are alternate ways of coping shaped by natural selection (Nettle, 2005). Thus, in any population, some individuals will have traits that help them deal with that environment, and some with traits that have a better chance of dealing with a different environment. There can also be traits that get in the way of coping with most environments. That is why natural selection promotes variability in personality. These variations support a "psychological immune system" that is sensitive to changing environmental demands (Tice and Baumeister, 2021).

Classifying Traits

Personality traits can most easily be measured by self-report questionnaires, which generate responses that can be grouped into domains using factor analysis.

Allport (1937), a pioneer in the development of personality theory, was the first to use the term "trait". But a British psychologist, Eysenck (1952) was one of the first researchers to develop a factor analytic system of personality. His model was based on three trait dimensions, two of which (extraversion and neuroticism) can still be found in the five-factor model of personality (FFM) (historically an expansion of the earlier three-factor theory). Eysenck's third dimension was misleadingly labeled "psychoticism" but is now divided into three other factors (agreeableness, conscientiousness, and openness to experience).

There have been many competing models of personality, each of which has advantages and disadvantages. But having to choose between so many competing options is confusing. More recent research shows that the five domains of the FFM best covers the ground of trait variation (Widiger, 2015). Thus, since the FFM is the most widely validated system, I will make use of that model throughout this book.

Today, most of the more popular systems in the past developed to describe personality profiles are no longer being used. For example, the 16 personality factors (16-PF, Cattell and Mead, 2008) were once influential, but are rarely applied to research or practice today, in part due to their complexity. After all, 16-PF are rather hard to remember, and it has long been known that a list of seven items is the maximum that most people can recall (Miller, 1956). In my view, there have been too many competing systems aiming to classify personality, and many are too complex to be of use in practice.

The developers of the FFM used factor analysis to define five overall domains. But are five too few? The FFM cuts this Gordian knot by describing subfactors called "facets" within the five broader domains. These 30 facets are less often used, either in research or clinical practice.

Only one of the older systems is still being applied, the Minnesota Multiphasic Personality Inventory (MMPI), which will be discussed in Chapter 3. Even so, the FFM covers all of the same territory, and is a strong predictor of functioning and psychopathology (Selborn et al, 2008). That is why I support this model, as well as those that closely resemble it.

The FFM Model of Personality

The developers of the FFM began with a unique way of describing traits. They used a "lexical" method, listing all words in the dictionary that can be used to describe personality, and then developing items that draw on them to create a questionnaire. A factor analysis conducted by Goldberg (2013) found that the best fit was for five domains. The FFM has gone on to be used to describe both normal personality and psychopathology. Credit for this long-standing research program goes mainly to two psychologists: Rooert McCrae and Paul Costa (2013). Some of its current leaders belong to groups led by (or trained by) Thomas Widiger (2015).

The FFM has an enormous amount of research supporting it, with at least 2000 published papers. There have been attempts to use a model with six factors instead of five (Feher and Vernon, 2021), adding an extra domain called "honesty-humility", but only a few personality researchers see a necessity to do so. There are some traits that have been researched but are not tracked by the FFM model. One is narcissism (Orth et al, 2024), which will be discussed in Chapter 8. A related concept is a "dark triad" (narcissism, Machiavellianism, and psychopathy), but these traits are more closely correlated with facets of the FFM than with its larger domains (Kowalski et al, 2021).

One possible limitation of the FFM could be that since it was validated in community populations, its scores might not account for pathological extremes. That is not a fair criticism. Commenting on another system for scoring the dimensions of PDs (Livesley et al, 1998), Widiger (1998) noted that four out of its five factors were identical. The same can be said for the Alternative Model for Personality Disorders (AMPD; Hopwood et al, 2018), which replaces openness with psychoticism, as well as the current edition of the International Classification of Diseases (ICD-11; World Health Organization, 2018), which does not have a scale for openness.

The Diagnostic Assessment of Personality Pathology (DAPP; Livesley et al, 1998) and the Schedule for Nonadaptive and Adaptive Personality (SNAP; Clark, 2007) are trait-based systems that also resemble the FFM (Aluja et al, 2024; Crego and Widiger, 2020). These tools have mainly been used in research.

We can safely conclude that the trait domains in the FFM are the most valid measure of personality we have, and that disorders of personality are generally amplifications of these profiles. The five factors overlap to some extent, and some moderating effects emerge from their interactions. But I will begin by considering each of them separately, summarizing their descriptions in standard texts (Widiger, 2015).

What the FFM Tells Us about Individual Differences

Extraversion describes high levels of social interaction that lead to greater sociability and assertiveness. This domain describes the extent to which individuals need to be around and interact with other people. Extraversion can be adaptive, given that it is associated with stronger social connections. But extreme levels of extraversion can be problematic if they lead to constant attention seeking, an inability to be alone, or taking too many risks. Also, the relationships of extraverts may be superficial. At the other end of this spectrum, *introversion* describes a preference for internal rather than external responses. This trait can be adaptive if those who have it find the right niche. But introversion can be problematic when it leads to social isolation.

People need to find the right niche to match their preferred level of social connection, that is, whether their personality tends toward extraversion of introversion. Those who require constant contact with other people, as well as those who prefer to spend more time alone, can find careers and intimate relationships that match those needs. This is probably why there is only a relatively weak relationship between this factor (or more precisely with its extremes) and a risk for psychopathology.

Neuroticism is a trait describing a tendency to have negative emotions and to be more reactive to stressors. It can be adaptive under conditions in which real threats need to be recognized at an early stage. Low levels of neuroticism would describe *emotional stability*. High levels of neuroticism can be a handicap in benign environments—if every setback or disappointment leads to anxiety, depression, or other dysregulated emotions.

This helps explain why higher neuroticism is associated with so many mental disorders. It is by far the most important trait for the study of psychopathology and for clinical practice (Widiger and Oltmanns, 2017). It describes how easily people get upset, how severe the upset is, and how long it takes to recover from it. Yet this trait remains in the gene pool, since being vigilant about stressors or potential threats has been essential for human survival. (Keep in mind that human history has been marked by all kinds of dangers.)

Agreeableness describes a tendency to be cooperative and friendly with other people. This trait is usually adaptive, because it supports the maintenance of social networks. But when agreeableness is overly strong, it can be maladaptive, particularly when there are good reasons *not* to trust other people. Predatory relationships usually require one person to be overly agreeable. At the other end of this spectrum is *antagonism*, which describes a tendency to be in frequent conflict with other people. This is usually a problematic trait, as it interferes with well-functioning interpersonal relationships.

Conscientiousness describes being hard working, organized, disciplined, and persistent. Conscientiousness is particularly necessary for success in a competitive modern world. This trait is adaptive in most environments and is rewarded by other people. If conscientiousness is not too high, this trait will have a positive impact on functioning. But when too extreme, it can lead to problems in work and relationships; rigidity and perfectionism can become problematic.

The other end of this spectrum describes *impulsivity*, which describes acting on whims without reflection. This is a trait that can lead to serious dysfunction in work and intimate relationships. Not being conscientious is associated with a wide range of impulsive behaviors that lead to negative consequences.

Openness to experience describes curiosity and a need to explore novel experiences. This trait is less important for understanding psychopathology. People who are highly curious and willing to try new things can be entirely functional. Some people are open to novelty, while others prefer to follow routines. Thus, variations on this trait are compatible with all sorts of life choices. But too strong a level of openness can be associated with poor judgment. And those who are *closed* to new experience may be missing out on pleasures in life.

The Facets of the FFM

Let us now briefly unpack each of the five factors by briefly describing their facets (Widiger, 2015). Each of the facets is "bipolar", in that they can be described as high or low on a spectrum. Differences in scores of personality traits offer a more detailed account of the FFM profiles.

Extraversion:

1 Warmth—The degree of displayed affection and closeness in relationships
2 Gregariousness—The tendency to seek the company of others
3 Assertiveness—The degree of dominance in social relationships
4 Activity—The level of energy and activity in daily life
5 Excitement seeking—The need for thrills and intense stimulation
6 Positive emotions—The tendency to be happy, excited, and cheerful

Neuroticism:

1 Anxiety—Proneness to worry and rumination
2 Angry hostility—The readiness to experience frustration, anger, and bitterness
3 Depression—The tendency for guilt, sadness, loneliness, and hopelessness
4 Self-consciousness—Sensitivity in social situations, such as ridicule, rejection, or awkwardness
5 Impulsivity—The ability to tolerate frustration and to control urges, cravings, and desires
6 Vulnerability—The ability to cope with stress

Agreeableness:

1 Trust—The general level of wariness or suspicion in contact with other people
2 Straightforwardness—Degree of sincerity or shrewdness
3 Altruism—Active concern for the well-being of others
4 Compliance—Inhibiting vs. expressing aggression toward others in conflict
5 Modesty—Degree of humility vs. arrogance
6 Tender-mindedness—Propensity to empathize with others

Conscientiousness:

1 Competence: Belief in one's own capacity to handle life's many challenges
2 Order—Degree and neatness and orderliness
3 Dutifulness—How strongly ethical principles guide action
4 Achievement striving—Aspiration level, the willingness to work toward goals
5 Self-discipline—The ability to follow through on tasks despite boredom
6 Deliberation—Long and careful thought

Openness:

1 Fantasy—Proneness to imagination, day dreaming, and creating
2 Aesthetics—Appreciation for beauty in art, music, poetry, nature
3 Feelings—Receptivity to and intensity of experienced emotions
4 Actions—The tendency to choose novelty over the familiar
5 Ideas—The degree of interest and curiosity in entertaining new thoughts
6 Values—The willingness to re-evaluate norms and values

Personality and Temperament

Temperament defines distinctive patterns of feelings and behaviors that originate in biological variations and that appear early in development (Kagan, 1998). While research on personality and temperament arise from different traditions, they describe much the same phenomena. Temperament can even be assessed to some extent in infancy but is less stable at that stage than personality traits in adults. Rutter (2005) noted that while temperament depends on factors that can be observed from birth, it interacts with environmental challenges to yield stable trait profiles later in childhood. In this way, trait profiles are driven by gene–environment interactions.

Temperament is mainly genetic in origin but can also be influenced by neurodevelopmental processes prior to birth (Mitchell, 2018). The complexity of neural migration to form stable synapses, beginning in utero and continuing over the course of childhood, creates a potentially random element and is not entirely predictable. This process, as well as differences in life experiences, helps explain why monozygotic twins are not entirely identical.

In summary, while temperament is at the root of personality, it tend to be described in a different way in the research literature. We no longer use the ancient Greek theory associated with Hippocrates and Galen, which described people as sanguine, choleric, melancholic, or phlegmatic—even if some of these terms remain in common parlance. Instead, modern research on the heritable component of personality is based on systematic observations and longitudinal follow-up studies of infants and young children.

A leading researcher in temperament (Rothbart, 2011) classified temperament based on a factor analysis of ratings on a questionnaire given to caretakers and confirmed these findings in a laboratory for behavioral testing. Rothbart identified three temperamental clusters: surgency, extraversion, negative affectivity, and effortful control. *Surgency* is defined as cheerfulness, responsiveness, and sociability. This domain closely tracks the FFM domain of extraversion and is a temperament that most parents find rewarding. *Negative affectivity* tracks the FFM domain of neuroticism and is a trait that most parents find difficult. Difficulties in managing emotions may be associated with shyness, a temperamental profile that Kagan (1998) called "behavioral inhibition". *Effortful control* describes the abilities to voluntarily manage attention and to inhibit or activate behavior. This trait more or less tracks the domain of conscientiousness.

While temperament can be identified in infancy, differences in the first year of life are not always predictive of later development. One reason is that human infants are highly neotenous, that is, more like a fetus than a child. Their repertoire of behaviors is more reactive than proactive. For this reason, most research on temperament has been conducted in middle childhood (ages 6–12). By that stage, one can speak of personality and apply the same model to describe them (Spengler et al, 2012).

One problematic type of temperament, "behavioral inhibition" (Kagan, 1998) describes a tendency to be anxious and to withdraw when faced with novel environments (White et al, 2011). This trait is a form of neuroticism, and can be a precursor of social anxiety later in life (Tang et al, 2020). Thus, extreme forms of temperament in infancy have an ability to predict psychosocial outcomes decades later.

Clinical Applications of the FFM

There have been many models for the classification of personality traits, each with somewhat different domains. But the FFM is easy to understand because it uses plain language with which most of us feel comfortable. That advantage reflects the origins of the system in lists of all words used to describe personality (Goldberg, 2013). The very large body of research the FFM has stimulated was summarized a decade ago in a Handbook (Widiger, 2015). If you have trouble remembering all five factors, you can use an acronym (OCEAN) built, in a different order, from the first letter of each one.

Let us consider some examples of how the five factors affect psychological development.

Extraversion and Introversion

Case 1 (High extraversion):
Roxane was a young woman with many friends and an active social life. People who knew her found her as talkative and charming. Living in a seacoast town, she worked on a fishing boat, but did not think this job was in any way dangerous. As a student, she would study for examinations in crowded and noisy cafes. In her off hours she enjoyed spending evenings talking with old friends, and had no problem in meeting new people.

Case 2 (Low extraversion):
Jonathan was a man in his 30s who like to be alone and who chose to limit his social activities. He lived alone and his job in a library allowed for little contact with co-workers. Jonathan spent a lot of time on the web reading. He had always been shy, and kept just one best friend from his school days, with little interest in finding a partner or starting a family.

Neuroticism and Emotional Stability

Case 3 (High neuroticism):
George was an engineer in his 30s who had always been a worrier and a pessimist. Even as a child he was prone to brooding about the present and anticipating that the future could be even worse. As an adult, he was able to follow a career path but was unable to commit to an intimate relationship. At his best, George dealt with his feelings by using black humor. However, his chronic anxiety had already taken a toll on his health, and he was sometimes dangerously close to becoming an alcoholic.

Case 4 (Low neuroticism):
Sandra was a middle-aged widow with two grown children. She had faced significant challenges in her life but always felt that things would eventually turn out right. She grieved the death of her husband but accepted the consequences without expecting further disasters. She successfully made use of extended family and a wide social network to provide emotional support. Sandra was also committed to a career as an administrative assistant in a large hospital.

Conscientiousness and Impulsivity

Case 5 (High conscientiousness):
Kyle was a successful lawyer. But he often worried that he could be performing below par and was usually the last person to leave the office. His wife sometimes complained that his high standards for her (and himself) interfered with their relationship, but she knew she could always count on him.

Case 6 (Low conscientiousness):
Lois was a single woman who had a life-long problem with controlling her impulses. She would shop online and run up debt on a credit card. Her schedule was often interrupted by distractions. She never finished university due to procrastination. However, Lois found a stable online job in information technology that did not require precise booking of appointments.

Agreeableness and Antagonism

Case 7 (High agreeableness):
Maria was a young woman who worked as a secretary. She could be described as a people pleaser and was popular within her social circle. While she could be disappointed when others did not return the many favors she did for them, Maria looked after her husband and children with warmth and emotional support.

Case 8 (Low agreeableness):
Kathy worked as an administrator in a bank but had a history of moving from one job to another almost every year. She attributed this to having to work in a "toxic environment", but her co-workers found her short temper and sarcasm to be difficult. Kathy remained single because she always found fault with every man she dated.

Openness to Experience

Case 9 (High openness):
Carl was a middle-aged journalist who had traveled the world for years. He sought out work that included a good deal of travel, and sought out exotic restaurants. His romantic partners almost all came from entirely different cultures. Carl had a roving eye in intimacy and never quite settled down with one person, and he invested more in his career.

Case 10 (Low openness):
Beverley was a middle-aged woman living in the same house where she grew up. She cared for her parents in their old age but saw no need to move out once they were gone. Beverly was satisfied with her a job at a local bank but never asked for a promotion. She did not travel and spent her vacations looking after the house. She was satisfied with a social life which centered on a group of women who met weekly over many years to play bridge.

I have chosen examples in which the pattern of FFM trait profiles is clear. Chapter 9 will examine their effects in clinical practice. The next chapter will describe how personality affects the life course.

Chapter 2

Personality over the Life Course

The Stability of Personality over Time

Personality traits are generally stable over time. This has been shown by longitudinal research in large community populations using the FFM (Terraciano et al, 2009). Its personality domains evolve only to some extent over the life course, and its core characteristics change little. While personality becomes more stable later in childhood, it can go through a period of destabilization during adolescence (McCrae and Costa, 2013). This is partly due to changes in hormone level. Also, until age 25, the brain is still growing and pruning unneeded synapses (Lebel and Beaulieu, 2011). The stability of the FFM domains only grows stronger in young adulthood, middle age, and old age (Terraciano et al, 2009). This trajectory reflects increased maturity of the brain connectome, possibly due to better cortical control over subcortical structures.

It is not true, however, as the 19th-century psychologist William James (1890) thought, that character is "set like plaster" by the age of 30. Rather, while personality development slows as we age, it can still happen. There is also evidence showing that life transitions, good or bad, can shift the level of some FFM domains, even as overall profiles remain stable (Roberts and Damian, 2019). If that were not so, then therapy designed to modify traits to increase functionality could not be effective. Most patients do not require a radical overhaul but a tune-up.

With time, some changes in trait profiles can be clearly beneficial. Thus, most people become more agreeable and more conscientious in middle age (Roberts and DelVecchio, 2000). One of the most beneficial changes over the lifespan is that neuroticism declines after age 30 (McCrae et al, 2000). Of relevance for clinical work, this observation helps explain why mental disorders that are related to dysregulated emotions, such as borderline

DOI: 10.4324/9781003519942-2

personality disorder (BPD), begin in adolescence but gradually remit with maturity (Zanarini, 2019).

In combination with increases in agreeableness and conscientiousness, a decrease in neuroticism indicates that most people evolve to function better in middle age (Niven, 2022). While we sometimes idealize youth, with its sense that anything is possible, it can also be a time of turmoil. Many mental disorders that are marked by impulsivity, such as substance use (Fleury et al, 2016), tend to remit as people grow older, possibly due to processes rooted in a greater maturity of the brain.

Personality across Cultures and Genders

A large body of research shows that FFM personality profiles are similar in cultures all over the world. McCrae and Terraciano (2015) reported that by and large, the FFM yields similar data in the developing world as in developed societies. Average personality profiles in 51 cultures are only partially affected by geographical and cultural variables, and differences that could be observed were unrelated to any kind of national character. Thus, the views of past anthropologists, who spent short periods of time living in other societies, and who claimed that societies have common personality structures (Freedman, 1999), have not been confirmed by empirical data. As McCrae and Terraciano (2015) point out, maturational patterns of overall trait profiles over time, as well as sex differences, show cultural invariance. The most variable FFM domain is openness, possibly due to the narrower range of options in more traditional societies.

The study of personality has implications for explaining clinically important gender differences in personality and psychopathology. Women are generally higher in neuroticism and agreeableness. Neuroticism probably accounts for the well-established fact that females are more likely to develop depression and anxiety, particularly given that most women are caretakers who cannot afford to ignore threats if they need to protect their children. Thus, the heritability of this trait makes sense in an evolutionary context (Campbell, 2020).

Women around the world are also higher in openness, agreeableness, and conscientiousness (Lockenhoff et al, 2024). Agreeableness is often useful, but most therapists will have had to address problems in women who come to treatment for problems with interpersonal relationships—all too often after choosing the wrong kind of partner for intimacy. Being too agreeable runs the risk of being exploited. In contrast, men are more troubled by losing social status, tending to be less bound to close relationships and to have more externalizing symptoms such as substance abuse

(Campbell, 2020). Men are also much less likely to seek psychotherapy (Vogel and Heath, 2016).

Although the personality differences between men and women are not large, they are consistent across many cultures. Notably, differences in trait profiles between the sexes are *larger* (not smaller) in countries which value egalitarianism for women (Lockenhoff et al, 2014). This might seem paradoxical, but they support the view that sex differences are innate, and that they emerge more clearly when social roles become flexible. Once again, we cannot personality without considering its heritability.

Personality and Success in Life

Does personality predict health and longevity? Do traits predict the quality of intimate relationships as well as divorce? Does personality predict occupational attainment? The answer to all of these questions is *yes*.

A review of longitudinal studies that have followed subjects for years found that positive trait profiles predict all these outcomes (Kern and Friedman, 2015). The strongest associations are with low neuroticism, high conscientiousness, and high extraversion. This is a combination of traits that best supports social functioning (Atheron et al, 2014; Roberts and Yoon, 2022; Roberts et al, 2007). In contrast, high neuroticism and low conscientiousness are predictors of reduced longevity. This profile can also be associated with suicidal behaviors (Brezo et al, 2006; Mann, 2000).

In a UK birth cohort study, traits measured in youth (higher extraversion and lower neuroticism) predicted mental wellbeing and life satisfaction 40 years later (Gale et al, 2013). A systematic review of many other studies found that these FFM domains, as well as higher conscientiousness, strongly predicted well-being, that is, how satisfied people are with their lives (Kern and Friedman, 2015). Moreover, these profiles do at least as well in predicting life outcomes as socioeconomic status or cognitive abilities. While there are exceptions, these relationships fall in the same range as those reported by most research in psychology and medicine.

The strongest correlations between trait domains and success in life are associated with high conscientiousness, which is by far the best predictor of success in a career (Heilmayr and Friedman, 2020). The other domains tap into how readily people access support in social networks. Higher levels of extraversion play a smaller role in a career but support social connections. High levels of neuroticism lead to emotions of anxiety and behavioral avoidance that are more likely to stand in the way of forming these connections. And it goes without saying that people who are more agreeable are more likely to have strong social networks, in or out of intimacy (Shiner, 2019).

It has been long been thought that socioeconomic level is the main factor holding back individuals from achieving life goals (Glymour et al, 2014). That is true to some extent, but personality is just as important. Resilience research shows that people who were raised in dysfunctional families can compensate for a bad environment if they have positive personality traits (Ayoub et al, 2018). These traits support social mobility and resilience and can eventually move people to a higher socioeconomic level. This is an important finding for clinicians, who may assume that socioeconomic deprivation is one of the main reasons why people who grow up in bad neighborhoods are at greater risk for psychopathology.

Personality and Health Psychology

Health psychology is a research domain that has generated a large body of research that gives weight to the importance of personality (Abraham et al, 2024; Luo et al, 2022; Marks et al, 2024).

Medical illnesses have many causes. Personality profiles are only one of many risk factors but sometimes lead to a tipping point (Johnson and Acabchuk, 2018). As these authors note (page 218), health psychology based on personality assessment has an important role to play in chronic illness,

> ... behavior change is the key target to help reduce the immense public health burden of chronic lifestyle illnesses. Health psychology also focuses on how social patterns influence health behavior and outcomes, in the form of patient-provider interactions or as social forces in communities where people live, work, and play. Health psychology is congenial to other health sciences, especially when allied with ecological perspectives that incorporate factors upstream from individual behavior, such as networks linked to individuals (e.g., peer groups, communities).

Thus, trait profiles also affect the way people deal with illness, especially chronic diseases (Stanton et al, 2007). Some traits, especially impulsivity, need to be addressed. But as shown by research on motivational interviewing (Miller and Rolnick, 2012), even though treatment for this population can be lifesaving, behavioral change promoted by health psychology requires highly skilled therapy. If it were not difficult to get people to give up alcohol, tobacco, and other drugs, these substances would not be addictive as their reputation shows.

Personality and Longevity

Longevity is a good marker for measuring health outcomes. Conscientiousness has the strongest relationship of personality profiles to how long people live (Kern and Friedman, 2015; Turiano et al, 2020). Research also finds a link between neuroticism and longevity (Roberts and Yoon, 2022). But "healthy neuroticism", that is, the avoidance of danger (Turiano et al, 2020) point in a different direction by showing the positive side of this domain.

Prior to the development of the FFM, one of the most famous personality patterns that has been hypothesized to be associated with any medical illness is a "type A" profile. But this relationship, once widely held by clinicians, has failed to be confirmed by empirical data. The original idea was that competitiveness, time urgency, and workaholism carry a risk for coronary artery disease, especially when compared to its opposite, "type B" (Friedman and Rosenman, 2020). More recent research described a "type D" profile, which describes high neuroticism (Kupper and Dennollet, 2018). That trait has sometimes been associated with increased vulnerability to medical illnesses (Mols and Denollet, 2010), but does not seem to shorten the life span.

Individuals with high neuroticism react to stressors more intensely, compromising defenses against illness. Moreover, impulsivity makes it more likely that those who have such traits will be exposed to stressors. Finally, people with low conscientiousness are more likely to abuse substances and become obese, seriously challenging their health status. In a famous longitudinal study of gifted children that followed its subjects for a lifetime, conscientiousness was a strong predictor of longevity, while impulsivity predicted a shorter life span—above and beyond specific risks such as substance abuse and proneness to accidents (Friedman et al, 1995). It is well established that diagnoses of impulsive PDs are associated with decreased longevity, often with a loss of at least ten years (Fok et al, 2012).

Thus, conscientiousness has a protective effect on health. People who are more impulsive and less conscientious are more likely to fail in their occupational and social roles.

Traits that have long-term associations with adult health can be identified in children (Friedman et al, 1995). That finding is consistent with the stability of personality over time and might suggest to some that clinicians consider intervening earlier in development to modify these profiles. But that is only a guess—we do not know whether therapy in childhood can significantly change personality.

Why Personality Predicts the Life Course

Humans are highly social animals. We live in families and social groups that provide us with connections and an identity. Our species has not evolved to live alone, and social networks provide the psychological oxygen necessary for flourishing and well-being. That is why mild levels of extraversion, which promotes interpersonal relationships, as well as a certain level of agreeableness, tend to be beneficial. Much the same can be said about having. Conscientiousness promotes sociality, since other people observe it and trust those who are most reliable. In contrast, a high level of neuroticism works against intimacy. By and large, other people find anxiety and depression difficult to deal with, so that fear and avoidance may eventually lead to social isolation.

In summary, personality is the hidden risk factor that explains why people develop all kinds of psychological problem, as well the specific pattern of psychopathology for which they are at risk. It is also a major factor in whether people fall ill and whether they have a longer life span.

Chapter 3

Personality Assessment

Advantages and Disadvantages of Formal Personality Assessment

Let us now consider how clinicians can assess personality in daily practice. Most mental health practitioners are trained to recognize trait profiles from clinical interviews. But although we can identify certain traits from personal histories, without a well-defined structure for doing so, these assessments can be idiosyncratic. We may also fail to pick up relevant data on historical events or current levels of functioning.

In the past, formal testing of trait profiles was central to the identity of clinical psychologists. Today, personality assessment is more likely to be the province of research projects for which psychometrically validated tools are required. However, formal assessments can offer additional information helpful for clinical work.

I am recommending the use of the FFM, the most thoroughly researched method for assessing normal and abnormal personality (Widiger and Crego, 2019). Given that the models used in ICD-11 and Section III of *DSM-5-TR* are similar to the FFM (see Chapter 8), I consider them to be good alternatives.

Personality assessment can be augmented by well-validated self-report measures. For dimensional scores, that involves having patients fill out self-report questionnaires. We can also use the FFM to assess pathological personality traits and full-blown PDs (Widiger et al, 2012).

While all these procedures add important information, time and money limit the availability of formal assessment. A large-scale survey found that assessment using standardized instruments is now much less frequent in clinical practice. The main exceptions are forensic settings (where the results of testing may be presented as evidence), or inpatient settings (where time is less of a constraint). Given these constraints, one can use brief versions of assessment tools.

These days, formal personality assessment remains more important for research, a domain in which clinical judgments are not readily trusted,

DOI: 10.4324/9781003519942-3

and in which validated measures are expected and required. Moreover, clinicians may not have formal training in this kind of assessment, and/or access to psychologists who have these skills. The use of psychological tests requires expertise, as well as payment for the time it takes to interpret them. I work in a hospital, and due to long waiting lists for assessments, we rarely request formal psychological testing.

Nonetheless, a vast literature on personality assessment has emerged over several decades (Corr and Matthews, 2020). Several academic journals are devoted to this research domain. Yet few of the tests on the market are used on a routine basis. They can best be considered as an adjunct to clinical judgment.

Yet when feasible, formal personality assessment has advantages. Standard self-report questionnaires yield quantitative data that describe trait profiles and can also be used to measure changes during or after treatment. That allows for what might be called a "personalized" approach (Zilcha-Mano, 2021). The data generated by formal testing raises different questions from interviews and can correct for clinician biases. By and large, a categorical diagnosis of a PD is too fuzzy to be sufficient, since people with the same diagnosis can have very different problems in life. However, as we will see, some categories are known to have specific evidence-based treatments.

Psychological testing can also be used to assess important symptoms. For example, research has attempted to use formal testing to assess suicidality. Based on clinical assessment and on machine learning, found that testing can identify suicidal ideation and predict future attempts. But that is not the same thing as predicting suicide, which remains an elusive goal in clinical practice (Paris, 2024). In any case, suicidal ideas are too common to be useful predictors of fatality. The reason is that death by suicide is very rare when compared to the high frequency of attempts, and the even higher prevalence of suicidal ideation. Moreover, the same information, based on standard questions in clinical evaluations, could have been obtained by a careful interview.

In summary, formal psychological testing is a different procedure from making a diagnosis and provides different information. To obtain reliable data requires well-validated self-report measures. By and large, however, these results tend to confirm what can be observed in a good interview. It is not that difficult, for example, to recognize high levels of neuroticism in the patients seen by clinicians.

Why Projective Tests Are No Longer Used for Personality Assessment

Personality assessment has been around long enough to attract a degree of nostalgia. When I was an undergraduate, projective tests were popular, both in research and practice. There was always something mysterious (and attractive) about the inkblots used in the Rorschach Test.

One of the graduate students in the psychology department at my undergraduate university went on to devote his entire career to study the Rorschach test (Weiner, 2003). Yet after decades of research, including new ways to make this test more valid (Exner, 2003), this method still does not meet modern standards in psychology for psychometric validity and reliability (Wood and Lilienthal, 1999). There is also doubt as to whether the Rorschach is a more valid predictor of outcomes beyond what a good clinician can observe in an interview (Wood et al, 2000). These are the main reasons why the test is now rarely used. In over 50 years of my own psychiatric practice, even when working on a team with clinical psychologists at a publicly funded hospital, no one ever used this test. The Rorschach is a colorful byway in the long journey of psychological research, but it lacks validity.

One of my undergraduate professors in psychology devoted his career to another once-popular projective measure, the Thematic Apperception Test (TAT, Morgan, 2002). This test asks people to create stories based on ambiguous drawings of life situations, which can then be scored and interpreted as reflecting inner conflicts and problems. Yet today the TAT has almost entirely disappeared from clinical practice. Once again, the problem with projective tests of all kinds is that their interpretation is too subjective to be reliable (Lilienfeld et al, 2000). We can do better with self-report measures.

Personality Assessment: Then and Now

The most widely used self-report personality test in the past, still occasionally used in practice, is the Minnesota Multiphasic Personality Inventory (now the MMPI-3; Whitman et al, 2021). Although the MMPI was once considered a "gold standard" of personality assessment, it is much more rarely used today. For one thing, its results are complex. Its scales describe a wide range of normal and abnormal variations in personality profiles. But unlike the FFM, its profiles are not rooted in a theoretical model of personality, but in factor analysis alone, and do not have a close relationship to clinical diagnoses.

The MMPI is also limited by time—even it its revised form, it has 500+ questions that cannot be answered in less than an hour, even on a computer, and it can cost thousands of dollars to score the results. Moreover, the MMPI does not map the domains of personality in the same user-friendly way as the FFM, which covers much of the same ground (Levitt and Gotts, 2021). This helps to explain why the MMPI, in spite of decades of research, is no longer a widely applied clinical tool. I can still find articles using this test, especially in its revised form. But I do not know any psychologists who use it routinely.

The most common reason for psychological testing these days may not be personality traits, but evaluations of cognitive function. There is an important role for neuropsychological measures in the assessment of neurodevelopmental disorders such as attention-deficit hyperactivity disorder (Boyle et al, 2020). A battery of tests can also be used to provide confirmation for a dementia that has an unclear presentation at an early stage.

Unfortunately, when it comes to personality, symptoms can mask the effects of traits. That is why clinicians who do not assess traits, with or without formal testing, are missing something important. The influence of the DSM and ICD systems of diagnosis reflects the fact that patients complain about symptoms but not about traits. Clinicians who treat symptoms with medications and/or standard forms of psychotherapy tend to target symptoms. Yet formal testing goes beyond surface features such as anxiety or depression, symptoms that are rooted in trait profiles. This is why we need to evaluate personality as regularly as what patients present as problems.

Doing so can also help us recognize when patients have diagnosable PDs. If a patient meets criteria for borderline personality disorder (BPD), then specific methods of treatment may be required (Paris, 2020). That is not the case for any of the other PDs, but this diagnosis should not be missed.

For all these reasons, assessing both normal and pathological trait profiles in patients should be part of good clinical practice. That gives an advantage to the FFM, a measure that has been validated in both normal and clinical populations. This system tells you more about the person than diagnosis alone.

The Limits of Self-Report

Most assessments of personality depend on questionnaires that have norms and can be reliably scored. In the past, doubts have been raised about whether patients give honest answers to personal questions. To deal with this problem, another of my undergraduate professors developed tests with questions that had zero face validity (i.e., items with no obvious relationship to what they measure), but whose opacity was designed to prevent people from putting themselves into the best light. His view was that the absence of face validity does not matter, as long as responses can be validated by predicting a given outcome. As an exercise, we were asked to predict how student would do in their first year based on high school grades, an autobiographical essay, and scores on the test. A combination of personality test scores and high school performance did best.

But these days, most personality measures ask questions that are easy to relate to trait profiles. Some assessment measures, such as MMPI, include "validity scales" to detect inaccurate responses that arise from embarrassment. And some instruments also offer the option of giving parallel questionnaires to family members.

Research shows that most people have a reasonable level of knowledge about their own personality and can provide valid responses to questions about sensitive issues (Robins et al, 2007). That is because they see their own traits as normative. Those who are perfectionistic think that most people are sloppy. Those who are impulsive find other people to be boring. Those who are antagonistic may think that other people lack the courage to speak their minds. Even narcissists do not hesitate to reveal their perceived superiority to others, which they see as a fact rather than a problem. And some patients with antisocial traits can actually be proud of being clever enough to be successful at cheating other people.

Ultimately, a consensus has developed that whatever limitations are inherent in self-report, they are less severe than with current alternatives. Moreover, self-reports can be cross-validated by other types of measures using similar constructs (Paulhus and Vazire, 2007). That is why there are self-report measures on the market for various psychiatric diagnoses (depression, anxiety, substance abuse, PDs), but that need not be the main way to make a diagnosis.

In summary, self-report is a useful and practical guide to assessment. Most people tell the truth about themselves, even when they see their traits as more adaptive and less problematic than they really are.

Using the FFM in Practice

The standard self-report measure for scoring the five factors is the NEO Personality Inventory, 3rd revision (NEO-PI-3; McCrae and Costa, 2010). But again, the time it takes to complete is a problem. The NEO-PI-3 has 240 questions that require about 40 minutes to complete, plus at least another 15 minutes for scoring. Fortunately, lengthy questionnaires in psychology can usually be shortened without losing much in the way of reliability or validity. For the FFM, there is a 60-item version called the NEO-FFI (NEO Five-Factor Inventory; McCrae and Costa, 2010). With only 25% of the original items, it requires only 25% of the time needed to complete the longer version. But since this radically shortened measure has only 12 questions for each of the five factors, it cannot measure facets (not always a great loss in clinical practice).

We can also use measures that were originally designed to not only assess PDs but also provide a profile of normal traits that resemble the FFM. One is the Alternate Model for Personality Disorders (AMPD) in *DSM-5-TR*, which now has a strong research base (Hopwood et al, 2020). A second is the section of ICD-11 that replaces PD categories with a model that measures both normal and abnormal personality (Tyrer et al, 2019). Chapter 8 will describe these measures in more detail, while Chapter 9 will suggest how assessing the traits they describe can support choosing specific targets in psychotherapy.

Some Tentative Recommendations

In summary, I recommend formal assessments of personality when there is time to administer them. They provide more detailed information using brief versions of self-report questionnaires. But I am not convinced that we should give up on categorical diagnosis entirely. Like most phenomena in science, categories have fuzzy edges, while dimensions identify features that are transdiagnostic but cluster together and overlap. As physicists have concluded about waves and particles, we need both. This view may not satisfy anyone on either side of the battle between categories and dimensions. But personality is a more complex construct than a set of symptoms and requires an approach that acknowledges that complexity.

Chapter 4

Genetics, Neuroscience, and Personality

Individual differences in personality, like other traits, are rooted in biology. Traits of all kinds are partially heritable, most having close to half of their variance accounted for by genes. That is why the influence of life events on personality cannot be explained fully by histories of childhood or adult adversities. Personality traits can best be accounted for by gene–environment interactions. I will begin with the evidence for heritable factors shaping individual differences in personality development.

Behavior Genetics

How do we know that personality is heritable? That conclusion is mainly based on *behavior genetic* methods, a simple but powerful research tool. You need a large sample of identical and fraternal twins. Since monozygotic twins share the same genes, while dizygotic twins only share half of them, comparing the frequency of concordance for a trait between these populations provides a quantitative measure of heritability. These findings have been consistently confirmed by adoption studies comparing traits in biological and adoptive parents (e.g., Kendler et al, 2018).

Turkheimer (2000) described three "laws" of behavior genetics that follow from a large body of research findings. The first is that genetic influences make a substantial contribution to individual differences in almost all observable phenotypes. The second is that compared to genetic effects, being raised in the same family has a much smaller effect on individual differences in personality. The third is that a nontrivial portion of these differences can be attributed to environmental effects that are unique to each individual and are not accounted for by being raised in the same family.

These methods should be understood as applying to averages across populations. Traits in individuals need not always be 50% heritable—some will have a stronger genetic component, while others will have a larger environmental component. For this reason, it is wrong to claim that

DOI: 10.4324/9781003519942-4

personality trait variations are almost entirely biological, or that life experiences do not play any major role in their development. Plomin (2018) promoted this overstatement in a book promoting the idea that a genome is a "blueprint". It is more correct to see similarities in traits within a family as shaped by both genes and environment, with the understanding that heritable traits cannot be separated from the environment, given that they influence what does or does not happen in the life of each individual.

We do not know precisely how genes effect the development of traits. The differences found in twin studies are much larger than what can be estimated from studies of variations in the genome. This discrepancy has been called a "heritability gap". With the exception of rare Mendelian diseases, no single gene or small number of genes determine any human trait. Instead, many genes interact with each other, have multiple functions, can be turned on or off, and interact with the environment. They can be compared to instruments in a vast orchestra that are combined to produce unique effects.

In recent years, researchers have been able to examine the entire range of human genes using genome-wide association studies (GWAS; Abdellaoui et al, 2023). Yet when researchers examine alleles linked with any trait, genes are not associated with a small number, but with hundreds (or thousands) of alleles. This explains why searches for a single gene controlling complex traits have been almost entirely futile. One can calculate a polygenic risk score (PRS) from GWAS data to add up all associations. But doing so still accounts for only about 5% of the total variance in most traits. Thus, the heritability gap does not disappear.

It should not be surprising that genes lack a direct relationship with traits. Genetics is as complex as life itself. Moreover, the largest part of the genome is linked to regulation, and not necessarily to making specific proteins. These complexities do not allow for any kind of genetic determinism; the rare effects of classical Mendelian inheritance are exceptions. The best supported view is one of complex interactions between genes, and between genes and the environment.

Why Heritability Is Over-Estimated or Under-Estimated

In the last several decades, there has been enthusiasm among scientists (and the general public) about the implications of decoding DNA. Given the impact of the Human Genome Project, almost everyone now gives genetics its due. Yet one can exaggerate what can be inferred from a genome. Today, you can even have it examined for a fee, a procedure that estimates a statistical (but not causal) relationship with your ancestors. Keep in mind that relationships between variables can be statistically significant even when they leave most of the variance unexplained. That is why psychological research has moved away from reporting p values, which can be replaced by effect sizes or confidence intervals measured as standard deviations (Cumming et al, 2012).

These findings show that heritable factors are one of the main causes of individual differences in personality. But we do not understand the precise mechanisms by which the genome affects brain development.

Unfortunately, quite a few academics, particularly in the social sciences, have been hostile to the power of the genome. Most of these opponents of heritability are intellectuals among whom a majority fall on the left end of the political spectrum (Haidt et al, 2009; Inbar and Lammers, 2012). These academics do not want to believe in theories that contradict the idea that human nature and human societies can be perfected. They therefore oppose what they consider to be "genetic determinism", which they see as a way of further marginalizing the disadvantaged. They see genetics as an "essentialist" discipline that stands in the way of building a better society, while equating biological models of human nature with a patriarchy and authoritarian politics.

These academics favor what Pinker (2004) has called a "utopian vision" in which progressive radical changes in individuals and society are possible. They may also believe that their own research supports progressive social change. These intellectuals see the genome as a barrier to these hopes. For all these reasons, "progressive" academics favor a "standard social science model" which ignores genetics (Pinker, 2004, 2009).

This perspective is profoundly mistaken. You cannot study biology by limiting your data to what lies below the neck. The human brain, which has greatly enlarged in the course of evolution, is enormously complex, but is still shaped by natural selection. People are not "blank slates" written on by their environment. Culture and families also play a role in shaping the brain. But their effects can only be understood by their interactions with genes. Factoring heritability into human development need not in any way interfere with social progress.

This controversy is overwhelmingly political. Intellectuals critical of evolutionary psychology lack a background in biology and insist that humans are too different from other animals to be understood by their heredity. They do not accept the view of the biologist E. O. Wilson (AZ quotes, retrieved March 31, 2025): "The genes hold culture on a leash. The leash is very long, but inevitably values will be constrained in accordance with their effects on the human gene pool."

Pinker (2004) describes an alternative view of human nature he calls a "tragic vision". In this lens, since human societies will always be imperfect, social and political planning need to take imperfections in our brains into account. For example, although humans are social animals, we are more likely to protect close relatives than those who are not related to us. This is called "kin selection", as emphasized in a classic book by Dawkins (1976) which argued that genes, and not individuals, are the target of natural selection. Dawkins' view is that we can only make the world better by actively *combatting* our inherent and genetically shaped tribalism. Our task is to accept that human nature is not naturally "good" and can be responsible for many negative consequences in the absence of cultural norms. This is why utopian visions almost always lead to dystopias.

The power of the genome has also been underestimated in clinical psychology, where the role of the environment is predominant, and where the concept of gene–environment interaction has yet to be fully integrated into the world of practice. At the same time, psychiatry has lost sight of the psychosocial environment by drawing closer to medicine and emphasizing biology.

Both sides of this divide need to embrace interactions and complexity. The brain is the most complex structure in the universe, with 86 billion interacting neurons linked by trillions of synapses. Moreover, our brains are the product of human evolution over hundreds of thousands of years and cannot be explained by cultural variation. We can only maintain Utopian fantasies because neuroscience is at its beginning of its journey.

Complexity theory is a model in biology that aims to take these interactions into account (Öngür and Paulus, 2024). It shows why you cannot understand systems, especially in biology, by reducing the level of analysis to cells or neural synapses.

Evolutionary Psychology and Personality

Evolutionary psychology is a relatively recent domain of scientific research (Buss, 2024). It applies the principles of Darwinian natural selection to account for the most universal aspects of human nature, as well as individual differences in personality (Lewis et al, 2020). Its viewpoint focuses on adaptation (Barkow et al, 1992), that is, whether traits do (or do not) promote organisms passing on genes to their descendants.

We can apply these principles to personality traits in animals. The existence of similar trait variations in other species has also been supported by science. For example, personality traits in cats have been described by the "feline five"—neuroticism, extraversion, dominance, impulsiveness, and agreeableness (Litchfield et al, 2017). In fact, personality in non-human species can be accounted for models that resemble the FFM (Weiss and Gartner, 2015). These individual differences in animal behavior support the conclusion that variations in personality are partly biological, linked to alternative ways of responding to changes in the environment.

Evolutionary theory is universally applied to biology, as it accounts for both physical and mental variations between individuals. Yet its application to psychology has met with opposition based on ideological biases. The evidence is overwhelming that understanding the mind requires an interactive perspective. Yet what Pinker (2004a) calls the "standard social science model" continues to view social forces and childhood experiences as the main factors in human development.

One important example is resistance to the existence of sex differences in personality, a central feature of evolutionary psychology (Buss, 2024). These findings are quite robust, even if they upset those who need to deny meaningful psychological differences between the sexes. A great deal of evidence shows that men and women differ in personality traits, albeit with large areas of overlap (Campbell, 2020). On average, females score differently on all FFM domains, most particularly for higher agreeableness and neuroticism (Murphy et al, 2021). These differences may correspond to what have been called stereotypes, that is, that women have higher levels of traits associated with nurturance, such as agreeableness that tends to favor social functioning, while men have higher levels of traits associated with assertiveness and dominance.

Even so, stereotypes can have a real grain of truth. Keep in mind that these relationships are averages, not traits that one can expect in any man or woman. There is plenty of room in society for those who share some characteristics with the opposite sex. The effects of sex can best be viewed as overlapping distributions with major variations in any individual.

This is why one can be an evolutionary psychologist and strongly support feminism. And some of the most creative researchers in evolutionary psychology, such as Anne Campbell (2020) and Sara Blaffer Hrdy (2024), have been women. The crucial point is that since trait profiles for the two sexes overlap, many women have traits that are more frequent in men, and many men have traits that are more frequent in women (Campbell, 2020). That leaves plenty of room for people of either sex to find a niche that best fits their personality profile.

Applying an evolutionary model to personality is important because it helps to explain why traits can be dysfunctional in some contexts, but functional in others. Consider neuroticism, the domain most closely linked to psychopathology. It makes sense that women, who are usually the ones to raise children, need to worry more. If the environment is truly dangerous, being easily upset or afraid can be an asset. In most animals, males are more extraverted, take more risks, and have a shorter life span. Similarly, the world has room for both extraverts and introverts, for people who are less (or more) agreeable, and for those who are more (or less) conscientious.

In summary, the neuroscience of personality does not describe human destiny. Instead, it defines sets of characteristics that bend the twig of development, but that remain open to change under environmental influence.

Genetics and the FFM

The developers of the FFM viewed personality traits as being more based on heredity than on the environment. As McCrae et al (2021, p.173) concluded: "evidence for the endogenous nature of traits is supported by studies of behavior genetics, parent–child relations, personality structure, animal personality, and the longitudinal stability of individual differences". These conclusions remain valid today. We now can apply behavior genetics to support the innateness of personality traits. Moreover, as shown by evidence from longitudinal studies, correlations of parental behaviors with traits in children are typically low, while the FFM is valid across cultures around the globe (McCrae et al, 2000).

Behavioral genetic studies have shown that each of the factors in the FFM are close to 50% heritable (Vukasović and Bratko, 2015). Yet since every trait is shaped by complex interactions, we are again left with a heritability gap. In a large-scale GWAS study of neuroticism (Nagel et al, 2018), almost 600 sites for alleles linked to this trait domain were identified. Similar findings have emerged from research on the other FFM domains (van den Berg et al, 2016). Given this gap between behavior genetics and molecular genetics, we cannot yet describe the mechanisms behind the genetic influences on personality profiles.

Individual differences in personality traits must involve variations in the structure of neural networks, although trait variations can also be influenced by biological factors in utero, the time when neurons begin to migrate to form a connectome of trillions of synapses. Mitchell (2018) interprets the complexity of synaptic development by a model in which outcomes are not determined in advance. For this reason, randomness plays a role in brain connectivity. Along with variations in the fetal environment, these random effects help to explain why monozygotic twins are never entirely identical.

The presence of temperamental variations at birth also supports their basis in biology. As noted in Chapter 2, brain development is incomplete at birth, but continues during childhood, after which synapses are heavily pruned during adolescence (Kirkland et al, 2024).

The maturity of brain networks is only complete at around age 25 (Sigelman et al, 2018). In adult life, as traits become more stable, problems associated with them may persist. This can lead to as diagnosable PDs, characterized by high neuroticism, low agreeableness, and low conscientiousness (Widiger and McCabe, 2020). This mix of problematic traits, particularly when amplified by life adversities, leads to difficulties in managing the social environment.

Neuroscience and Personality

When I was a student, neuroscience was a new domain and even had a different name: "physiological psychology". Brain anatomy and the functions of neurotransmitters were poorly understood, so we were in no position to account for human universals or individual differences in behavior, emotions, or cognition. Today it is possible to begin to develop a neuroscience-based model of personality (DeYoung and Allen, 2019), even if future researchers will view it as provisional.

Thus far, imaging studies, as recently reviewed in detail, have allowed us to correlate brain activity in specific regions to a few mental disorders and personality profiles (DeYoung et al, 2022). The best evidence, once again, is for neuroticism, marked by excess activity in subcortical areas and decreased inhibition of emotion from the prefrontal cortex. As De Young et al (2022, p. 5–6): note:

> Numerous studies have shown that variations in the function of the amygdala and its brain region have an association with neuroticism. This finding has been supported by large studies of non-human primates, which provide evidence for a causal role of the extended amygdala in shaping individual differences in fear and anxiety. Finally, a negative correlation between neuroticism and cortical surface area has been found in meta-analysis and in multiple, very large human samples in a region of the dorsomedial prefrontal cortex that appears likely to be involved in self-reflection, emotion regulation, and the subjective experience of emotion. All of these findings are consistent with view that neuroticism can be like an alarm bell that goes off all too easily and that control switches from higher brain areas do not properly switch it off.

Another aim of neuroscience research has been to correlate personality traits with levels of brain neurotransmitters. Some studies have linked defects in serotonin activity with Neuroticism (DeYoung et al, 2022). But that cannot be the whole story. For example, antidepressants that promote serotonin reuptake at the synapse are only effective about half the time (Bschor and Kilarski, 2016). It has also been claimed that clinical depression and neuroticism are related to interaction between a serotonin transporter gene and adverse life events (Caspi et al, 2002). But it has been difficult to replicate these findings (Haberstick et al, 2016). This may be due to the complexity of neuroticism as a trait; this phenotype is a final common pathway for many risk factors.

Extraversion is the other FFM domain that has been shown to have neural correlates. It is related to a reward system in which dopamine is the main neurotransmitter (DeYoung et al, 2010). Thus, extraverted people are more likely to seek rewards, particularly those that come from interpersonal relationships, while those are highly introverted may eschew these rewards in favor of safety. But introversion of a moderate degree is consistent with normality: some people would rather read a book than go to a party. This trait can make some people socially isolated, but only at an extreme.

The neuronal correlates of the other three factors in the FFM are less clear. The domain of openness is usually consistent with normality. Those who are high in this trait are curious and imaginative, while those who are low can be narrow-minded. But openness has not been shown to have a consistent relationship with either specific brain regions or the activity of specific neurotransmitters.

Agreeableness and conscientiousness, in spite of their importance for social functioning, are not currently known to be correlated with differences in brain anatomy or neurotransmission (DeYoung et al, 2022). As we have seen, high levels of conscientiousness are the best predictor, after intelligence, of academic and occupational success, as well as of health-promoting behaviors and longevity. While extremes on this domain can risk disabling perfectionism, evidence for its neural correlates has been inconsistent.

Clearly, personality neuroscience has a long way to go. For now, it is limited by our weak understanding of the details of brain function. Since these processes, both at the anatomical and synaptic level, are highly complex, we need to be patient and not jump to premature conclusions. What does seem clear from the present state of research is that variations in personality have an important biological component. The next chapter will focus on how these trait profiles interact with the environment.

Chapter 5

Life Experiences, Personality, and Resilience

Adversity, Resilience, and Personality

The idea that life adversities, particularly during childhood, can shape personality and psychopathology has a long history, and that has often been taken for granted. But it is only partially correct. It is certainly true that adverse early experiences increase the *risk* for negative outcomes. But that is a statistical relationship that does not necessarily apply to individuals. Most people are resilient to adversity, and single traumatic events rarely lead to long-term consequences. Moreover, when the environment of childhood is dysfunctional, it tends to stay that way, leading to cumulative effects over years (Rutter, 2006).

The currently popular emphasis on trauma also fails to explain the ubiquity of *resilience*. In the course of human development, resilience is the rule, not the exception, and psychopathology is not the most usual outcome (Goldstein and Brooks, 2012; Rutter, 2012). A large body of research shows that only a minority of those exposed to childhood adversity are permanently affected (Paris, 2022a, 2022b). The most vulnerable are children who are highly sensitive to their environment (Belsky and Pluess, 2009) and who are higher in neuroticism.

Attributing psychological traits and/or symptoms to traumatic events in early life is an oversimplification of a complex and interactive process (Paris, 2022). It is more accurate to say that early adversity is most likely to affect those who are already vulnerable due to their personality profiles. Moreover, while heritable temperament plays a role in shaping vulnerability, temperament and personality can also shape positive traits that support resilience. That is why variations in personality have been naturally selected by evolution.

It should, therefore, not be surprising that resilience is the rule (Masten and Cicchetti, 2016). Our species evolved in environments in which death due to disease or predation was common. If those who survived childhood had not been resilient, our species would have long become extinct.

DOI: 10.4324/9781003519942-5

Resilience can be measured by research methods which show that it is strongly related to personality trait profiles (Rutter, 2006). Large-scale longitudinal studies in children have examined the outcome of adversity. One large-scale longitudinal twin study found that genes and environment make a roughly equal contribution to resilience (Amstadter et al, 2014). Similarly, Assary et al (2021), who followed a cohort adolescent twins into adulthood, found that half of the variance in their sensitivity to the environment was heritable, and that separate pathways process positive and negative experiences.

A follow-up of children at risk due to poverty (Werner, 2014) found that similar experiences can lead to entirely different outcomes, ranging from diagnosable psychopathology to the absence of measurable symptoms. In the UK, the longitudinal Isle of Wight Study found that resilience to early adversity was very frequent, and that later positive experiences could compensate for negative events (Collishaw et al, 2007a, 2007b; Rutter et al, 1976). In New Zealand, a large-scale longitudinal study found that most of those exposed to traumatic or neglectful environments did not develop mental disorders as adults (Fergusson, 1999), and that child abuse accounted for only 5% of outcome in adulthood on various domains of psychological functioning (Fergusson et al, 2011).

Resilience depends on what can be called a *psychological immune system* (Tice and Baumeister, 2021). This construct focuses on the processing of life events, governed by inherited temperament and personality traits (the result of interactions between temperament and experience).

Consider again Neuroticism, a key risk factor in personality profiles (Widiger and Oltmanns, 2017). This domain describes strong emotions in the face of adversity, and how long it takes people to get over these reactions. People high in neuroticism are less happy and more likely to develop mental disorders of all kinds. In contrast, people who are low in neuroticism can put adverse events out of their mind, and do not endlessly ruminate about them.

That is one reason why only 5–10% of people exposed to high stressful events develop post-traumatic stress disorder. On the other hand, highly neurotic people are better at protecting themselves, while higher levels of extraversion, agreeableness, and conscientiousness make it easier to find supportive social networks and helpful mentors when adverse events occur (Masten and Chicchetti, 2016).

There is also evidence from a metanalysis (Oshio et al, 2018) that *resilience* to adversity is related to a more positive FFM profile: low neuroticism, high agreeableness, and high openness. These traits help people to move past adverse events and find better ways of coping.

All these findings demonstrate the power of the genome and personality in the development of resilience. Rutter (2012) adds *luck* to this recipe and describes how finding meaningful attachments can become "turning points" in development. The effects of resilience are more likely to occur by connecting with the right people, going to the right school, and living in the right neighborhood.

This discussion does not deny that life experiences can play a major role in personality development—only that they do not, by themselves, reliably predict long-term outcomes. Clinicians tend to generalize from samples of patients who seek treatment for symptoms. They do *not* see people with much the same histories who are essentially asymptomatic. For this reason, their impressions, drawn from clinical experience are not representative of the population as a whole (Cohen and Cohen, 1984). Adults can also develop serious psychological problems in the absence of childhood adversity (Paris, 2022a).

Keep in mind that the relationship between life experiences and personality or psychopathology is statistical, not causal (Kessler et al, 1999; McKay et al, 2022). Risk is not the same as causation, and resilience is a function of traits. Those who are less neurotic, more agreeable, more extraverted, and more conscientious are more likely to find the resources needed to overcome adversity. Thus, personality sets boundaries on the extent to which good or bad life experiences modify trait profiles.

In research on highly sensitive children (Pluess et al, 2018), adversities were found to have a clear negative effect, but that those with high sensitivity were also more affected by positive experiences. This helps explain why traits that seem to be maladaptive are not eliminated by natural selection. Clearly, differences in response to the environment are of great clinical significance.

Heritable traits determine the thresholds at which life experiences have an influence on later development. People with different profiles can be referred to as *orchids* (high sensitivity), tulips (medium sensitivity), or as *dandelions* (low sensitivity). A book length essay has usefully applied this metaphor (Kennedy, 2013).

The principle that adversities have greater effects on those with high sensitivity to their environment does not mean that experience has no effect. Statistical risks do not apply in everyone exposed to adversity. Some are more sensitive to life events, whether they are good or bad. These discrepancies between risks and outcomes reflect how life experience is processed by traits. Sometimes luck also plays a role, when the environment takes a positive direction or offers an unexpected opportunity. But as an old saying puts it, opportunities come to the prepared mind.

In summary, research in developmental psychology rarely finds linear pathways that lead to predictable outcomes. This is mainly due to individual differences in traits that govern sensitivity to life events. If one finds a relationship between a risk and an outcome, even if it obtains statistical significance, such findings fail to account for a larger number of cases in which pathological outcomes are absent, or that the same outcome can emerge in the absence of risk factors. These principles define the sub-discipline of developmental psychopathology: when psychopathology does develop, it can reflect *equifinality*, that is, that the same result from different risk factors, as well as *multifinality*, that is, that different outcomes can arise from the same risks (Cicchetti and Rogosch, 1996).

Another problem is that research on the relationship between childhood environment and adult outcomes has often used imprecise measures of adversity, relying on fuzzy constructs such as "stress" or "trauma", which tend to distort or exaggerate their original meaning. These terms have been subject over time to *concept creep*, a process in which definitions expand to include phenomena that were not part of the original construct (Haslam, 2016).

Finally, life adversities are more pathogenic when they are multiple, leading to cumulative effects. This was one of the main findings of the Isle of Wight study (Collishaw, 2007a, 2007b). As Shakespeare had one of his characters say, "When sorrows come, they come not as single spies but in battalions".

Even when adversity is severe and multiple, resilience can still play a mediating role. In follow-ups of Romanian orphans who had been severely neglected during an infancy spent in very low quality orphanages, but when later adopted abroad into healthy families, most of these children did well in life (Rutter et al, 2007). While those who were adopted at a later age had more problems, this "natural experiment" demonstrated the likelihood of resilience when the environment changes.

Just as our immune system helps to protect us from disease, our psychological immune system prevents most of us from developing mental disorders (Tice and Baumeister, 2021). This system is based in heritable variations in trait profiles that govern the ability to process and contain the effects of adverse experiences.

Thus, vulnerability to mental disorders, or to psychological problems of any kind, cannot be understood outside the context of personality. These conclusions are supported by behavioral genetic research showing that growing up in the same family does not necessarily make children more similar to each other in personality.

These findings are also a useful antidote for the long-standing tendency of psychotherapists to blame parents and families for anything that goes wrong with children. Clinicians may change their minds when they raise their own children and observe how different they are from each other. Raising children is hard enough at is, without entering into what Furedi (2002) calls "paranoid parenting". These attitudes have been adopted by highly educated people, influenced by a "therapeutic culture" (Furedi, 2017). We may need to go back to a time when parenting was governed by a commonsensical respect for the human family.

How Much Do Families Matter?

I trained in psychiatry more than half a century ago. At that time, it was often assumed that the quality of parental care, almost without exception, has the most profound influence on personality development. My generation was good at blaming parents—until we raised our own families. In spite of being mental health professionals, we had to learn how difficult it is to meet unrealistically high expectations.

Some psychiatrists (particularly those who are biologically oriented) have gone in a different direction, tending to dismiss the effects of parenting on psychopathology. They have been particularly critical of theories that bad parenting was responsible for severe mental illnesses (e.g., Hobson and Leonard, 2001). They are right about schizophrenia and bipolarity. But their view of other mental disorders is simplistic.

In spite of a weak evidence base, this idea, that personality can be entirely explained by how parents raise their children is popular—but wrong. We need to consider other explanations. One is that parents and children share heritable problematic traits (Plomin, 2018). A related idea is that parents have more difficulty raising children with a difficult temperament. The best supported view is that failures in parenting are one of a larger set of interacting risk factors that statistically raise risk, but do not, on their own, lead to predictable outcomes.

Yet the view that parents are mainly responsible for the mental health of children remains influential. That is why I wrote a book entitled "Myths of Trauma" (Paris, 2023).

Judith Rich Harris (1997) was a psychologist who challenged most of the theories that blame parents for problems in their children. Her perspective drew wide attention from the educated public—and anger from many clinicians. Harris emphasized the centrality of experience outside the family, particularly in relationships to peer groups. Even Jerome Kagan (1998b), who always made a point of considering temperament, thought Harris went too far. Her ideas were sometimes caricatured as "parents don't matter" but might be better framed as "parents don't matter as much as you think".

Harris relied on evidence from behavior genetics supporting the conclusion that similarities between parents and children reflect a common heredity. The key finding is that, as shown by twin studies, half of the variance in personality is environmental, but growing up in the same family does not make siblings more similar, either in personality or in symptoms. Using the terminology of behavior genetics, the shared environment is less influential, and the unshared environment has more impact (Plomin, 2020).

It is certainly remarkable how children can be very different in personality from their siblings. The same environment leads to different outcomes because of differences in temperament. It has been said that parents of one child believe in the environment, while those have two children come to recognize the power of heredity (Zuckerman, 1987). We raise our children in much the same way, but find the results to be different.

Attachment Theory and Personality

I emphasize that simplistic theories that see parenting as the main driver of personality have not been confirmed by research, particularly data that considers heredity and temperament. But we need to consider an influential model that be claimed to point in a different direction. This is *attachment theory*, a set of hypotheses that have stimulated a very large amount of research. The attachment model, formulated by Bowlby (1979), may be the only theory of child development based on a psychodynamic model that has been subjected to systematic investigation, and that has gained support from empirical data

The key idea of attachment theory is that since children are born relatively helpless, they are programmed to attach themselves to a primary caretaker, usually the mother. Children then develop different "attachment styles", some of which can be problematic. The main styles are secure, anxious, avoidant, and disorganized. Fortunately, secure attachment is what we see in the majority of children.

It was originally assumed that people continue with the same attachment style in adulthood, but that is not always the case. Genes and environment can have different effects on attachment at different stages of life. These individual differences in adult attachment are also associated with FFM domains, particularly neuroticism, which are related to well-being in adult life (Marrero-Quevedo et al, 2019).

The question as to whether differences in attachment styles are genetic, environmental, or both, can be addressed by applying the methods of behavior genetics. While there have not been enough studies to conduct a metanalysis, we do have narrative reviews of this literature (Erkoreka et al, 2021; O'Connor et al, 2000; Oliveira and Fearon, 2019; Picardi, et al 2020). They show that, by and large, attachment styles, like almost all traits, are partially heritable, with genetic factors accounting for nearly half of the variance. Moreover, as is the case for other traits, genetic factors become more important later in adulthood than they are earlier in the life course. The data also shows that attachment styles and personality traits are linked, so that a secure attachment style is associated with lower neuroticism, as well as higher extraversion, openness to experience, agreeableness, and conscientiousness, while insecure attachment styles are linked to lower agreeableness and lower conscientiousness (Zarei et al, 2014).

We may, therefore, conclude that while secure attachment is associated with better mental health, these features are linked to personality trait profiles, which are in turn shaped by both heritable and environmental factors. These conclusions should make us cautious about claims that attachment theory proves that parents shape the personality of their children. The model needs to be updated to take into account how children with a difficult temperament are difficult for their caretakers. Thus, a large body of evidence contradicts the assumption that childhood experience is the primary driving factor in adult personality

Environmental adversities that emerge later in life can be just as important as earlier events (Bleidorn et al, 2014). Three general conclusions could account for symptoms with a later development. First, there is a strong and relatively stable genetic foundation for individual differences in personality that exists throughout the adult life span; second, that environmental influences become more important and contribute to an increasing stability of personality traits from early to middle adulthood; and third, that both genetic and nonshared environmental influences contribute to both stability and change in personality.

Equipped with this knowledge, one task for the next generation of research on personality development could be identify which of the FFM factors matter most. As we have seen, Neuroticism is the most important factor in psychopathology. But Conscientiousness continues to be protective against mental disorders, and its level generally increases in old age (Specht et al, 2011).

Sociocultural Factors and Personality

Is personality is shaped by cultural differences or social conditions? Research has shed some light on this question (Roberts and Yoon, 2022). Several theorists have emphasized the challenges of modernization, a social process that promotes individualism, replacing social roles predetermined by families and social networks with a bewildering range of life choices (Ingelhardt, 2020). Some trait profiles (such as high extraversion, high openness, and low neuroticism) may be favored by modernity, since they help people navigate complex environments. But other profiles (high neuroticism and low conscientiousness) require people to struggle more to find a niche and a social role. For example, an agricultural worker may easily find a place in a traditional rural society, while modern urban societies demand a set of skills that require training. Moreover, in a traditional society, people have less need to build unique life goals, while under modernity, what McAdams (2021) has termed a "narrative identify", needs to be created anew in every generation.

As we have seen, the Big Five Factors describe personality in all societies. There are a few differences, but they can be viewed as small. What differences have been found do not follow stereotypes about "national character" (McCrae and Terracino et al, 2015). Yet those who have a specific cultural background may believe in their own stereotype, even when FFM scores do not support such a perception. For example, the British do not typically have a "stiff upper lip" and are actually somewhat more extraverted than people in other countries (Kajonius & Mac Giolla, 2017). Thus, it would be a mistake to exaggerate minor differences in trait profiles, or to apply them to individuals who share a common culture.

But are there measurable individual differences in traits between social classes, racial groups, or culture? Scores on the FFM do not vary much under the influence of any of these factors (Widiger, 2017). But there is good evidence for the influence of sociocultural factors on psychopathology and personality disorder (Paris, 2020b). This while social risk factors may be downplayed in clinical practice, they play an important role in the risk for psychopathology.

The most consistent social risk factor for mental disorders is low socioeconomic class, which reduces opportunities and is associated with poor social support. For this reason, lower class life undermines resilience for those who are already vulnerable (Cockerham 2020).

A second predictor of psychopathology is "social defeat", often related to racial discrimination, which has been shown to raise the risk for psychosis in the UK and Western Europe (Selten et al, 2013). But even here personality plays a role, in that those with higher neuroticism could be more vulnerable to what has been called "social defeat" (Sturman and Mongrain, 2008).

A third predictor concerns, as discussed above, the greater individualism of modern society, an expectation that affects everyone. These values can be problematic for people who lack traits that could help them form a stable identity (Kitayama and Salvador, 2024.). In contrast, many cultures, particularly more traditional societies, tend to be collectivist, and have stronger structures promoting group and family identity. Even marriage is a choice for a family, and not for individuals. These cultures provide support to those who adhere to social norms, but not for those who are more individualistic. In contrast, societies that are more individualistic are supportive to those with higher ambitions but can create difficulties for those who lack traits associated with successful competition.

A fourth potential predictor is social contagion, in which behaviour, emotions, or symptoms spread through a social network. This mechanism is particularly important for adolescents who are most strongly influenced by peer groups, and it may account in part for the behavioral problems seen at this stage of development (Jarvi et al, 2013, Paris, 2024b). This process may be accelerated by modern technology, particularly when adolescents spent large amounts of time on social media (Haidt, 2024). Yet here too, personality traits such as Neuroticism may determine whether those who are exposed to longer screen times develop psychopathology (Alshamsi et al, 2015).

All this data seems to show that social stressors play a role in the development of personality and psychopathology. But it does not show that they do so in the absence of interactions with biological and social risk factors.

Suicide is a good example of how social differences influence behavior. As documented by the pioneer suicidologist Emile Durkheim (1951), and confirmed by contemporary research (World Health Organization, 2021), there are major variations across the globe in the frequency of death by suicide. Yet while suicide is linked to neuroticism and is known to have a heritable component of its own (Peters et al, 2018), most people with this profile never die by their own hand.

While the mean suicide rate across all countries is 9/100,000, there are large differences between European nations: Russia has a high rate of 21.6, while Greece has only 3.6. The long-held belief that suicide is more frequent in Sweden is untrue—the current rate there is 11.7, less than in the US. There are also differences between countries that have similar cultures: the US rate is 14.5 while Canada has only 10.3. Finally, even though we often hear claims that death by suicide is increasing, that is only true of the US, and rates have been decreasing in most countries worldwide (WHO, 2021). These cross-national variations must be at least partly based on social conditions. Personality cannot readily account for these findings at a population level. It is much more likely that trait profiles shape individual differences in sensitivity to life events that are at the core of so much psychopathology.

The next chapter will place all these risk and resilience factors into a single overall model of personality development.

Chapter 6

A Biopsychosocial Model of Personality Development

This brief chapter will attempt to bring together the effects of risk and resilience on personality into a single model. While mental disorders and personality disorders have been described using this theory, only a few have applied it to personality traits (Garcia, 2024; Savulescu et al, 2020).

Personality is a complex construct that is influenced by heredity, life experiences, and social context. That is why developing an interactive theory, as opposed to searching for single causes, is the most useful guide for clinicians. We need to adopt a broader, evidence-based view of personality and its effects on psychopathology. We also need to strike a balance between blaming genes, childhood adversities, or social disadvantages alone for problematic traits. Psychopathology does not usually develop unless many risk factors occur in the same individual.

With this goal in mind, I will offer a sketch of a *biopsychosocial* (BPS) model of personality that can be applied to both normal variations and pathological personality profiles.

The BPS model was developed by George Engel, an internist with a strong interest in psychosomatic medicine. This model is unique in that it takes into account the interaction of biological, psychological, and social factors in development. The BPS model was developed to understand medical illness, has been widely applied to health psychology (Bolton, 2023), and expanded to account for the complex causes of mental disorders (Engel, 1980).

Some critiques of the BPS model in psychiatry have seen it as vague or nonspecific. This criticism tends to be accompanied by the use of a traditional medical model, which some critics have termed as a "bio-bio-bio" theory (Whitley, 2014). But the BPS model is the most important theory of psychopathology that offers a fully interactive point of view (Bolton and Gillett, 2019).

It is worth emphasizing that a BPS model does not simply add up multiple risk factors but is based on interactions between multiple risk and

DOI: 10.4324/9781003519942-6

protective factors in development. It can be considered as an elaboration of older diathesis-stress models (Salomon and Jin, 2020). Multiple risk factors are needed to overcome what has been called a *psychological immune system*. That concept is also consistent with the idea of differential susceptibility to the environment (Belsky and Pluess, 2009). The model is also consistent with research showing that mental disorders are rarely associated with single genes, and that environmental risks do not have consistent effects unless they are severe and multiple (see reviews in Paris, 2022a, 2022b).

Thinking interactively is difficult. Our minds are generally more comfortable with single causes and linear pathways to outcomes. But with greater cognitive flexibility, we can avoid the temptation of attributing the causes of mental disorders to single risk factors. Existing data does not allow for that kind of simplification. Personality is complex in every way. Personality profiles describe what have been called "complex traits" (Gelernter, 2015), that is, phenotypes that are not fixed, but emerge from multiple interactions between genes and with the environment.

The BPS model also provides a framework that can explain the gap between risk factors and outcomes. These gaps are repeatedly found in systematic research. Studies that examine more than one or two independent variables, and that use multivariate statistics to measure interactions remain rare. The BPS model could encourage personality science to carry out research that measure biological and psychosocial risks in the same populations. Unfortunately, these domains have followed different research traditions and are almost always published in different scientific journals. The result can be that findings that are statistically significant are not strong enough for prediction, particularly in clinical populations. Finally, in view of the "replication crisis" that afflicts a good deal of research in psychology, we need larger samples that can tease out the effects of overlapping causal factors.

Reductionism and Emergence

The BPS model was developed to consider the complex causes of illness and designed to replace the *reductionism* that dominated 20th-century medicine. That point of view remains influential in the 21st century (Öngür and Paulus, 2024).

It must be acknowledged that reducing complex phenomena to a simpler level has often been a successful strategy in science. Much has been learned, for example, by examining biological phenomena using the techniques of physics and chemistry. On the other hand, biology itself tells us more about living things than either of these disciplines, and it has unique aspects, such as natural selection, that could not have been predicted by reduction.

Emergence is a property of complex systems (Gold, 2009). Put simply, the whole is usually more than the sum of its parts. Complex systems, like living organisms, cannot be fully understood without considering how they function at a higher level. This leads us to the concept of emergence, that is, that when systems are sufficiently complex, they have properties that cannot be predicted from their constituents. To consider a simple example, the properties of liquid water are not predicted by the characteristics of hydrogen and oxygen, or by the bond between them.

The errors of reductionism, and its failure to take emergence into account, have affected all aspects of psychological science, including individual differences in personality. For example, at the dawn of the neuroscience era, some thought that specific neural pathways and neurotransmitters could be associated with specific personality domains (Cloninger et al, 1993). But these hypotheses have earned little support from research.

Longitudinal studies of birth cohorts have been used to see if specific genes interacting with a negative environment produce psychopathology. Consider the Dunedin study, a longitudinal follow-up of a birth cohort of children in New Zealand who are now in middle age (Belsky et al, 2020). As discussed in Chapter 4, the much-quoted studies of this cohort have claimed that changes in genes for monoamine oxidase could be linked with antisocial behavior (Caspi et al, 2002), and that differences in alleles for serotonin transporter genes could be associated with depression (Caspi et al, 2003). However, attempts to replicate these findings have not consistently confirmed them (Kolla and Vinette, 2017). The reason is that it is unlikely that a single site on the genome could be implicated in the emergence of complex traits.

GWAS studies have now supplanted the search for "candidate genes". As discussed in Chapter 4, this method shows that hundreds of sites are associated with most outcomes, and that even when one finds a statistical association, it rarely accounts for a large proportion of outcome variance. The inability of current methods to identify specific mechanisms for gene–environment interactions should not, however, be discouraging. The systems under study are enormously complex and not yet well understood. Personality is a domain in which nature and nurture are intertwined and not easily separated.

A BPS model is useful for understanding how multiple factors, both for risk and for resilience, shape childhood temperament into a stable personality structure in adulthood. We need more research to show how these interactions actually work. But we first need to be comfortable with complexity.

Unfortunately, research still tends to look at biological and psychosocial risk factors in silos, instead of studying how they reinforce each other, or protect people with potentially problematic trait profiles from adversity. This reflects a tunnel vision that afflicts both those who are strictly biological, and to those who believe that early life experiences are what account for most psychopathological outcomes.

There are several reasons why clinicians and researchers get this wrong. One is that the patients who seek help are those who already had a predisposition to fall ill. We do not see the vast majority who are resilient and never succumb to mental disorders. A second reason is that research findings in psychology tend to report relationships that are only statistically significant. But statistical significance is not the same as causality. If your sample is large enough, you can find statistical relationships even when they only affect a vulnerable minority (Paris, 2022a).

Personality traits, since they are partly heritable and partly environmental in origin, straddle the great divide between biological psychiatry and clinical psychology. The more we think about a patient's personality, and avoid focusing exclusively on symptoms, the more likely we are to find complex interactive processes needed to account for personality development.

In this respect, a biopsychosocial model is the logical starting point for further research, and that should measure the effects of genes and environment in the same sample. This kind of research benefits from longitudinal follow-ups, some of which studied twins in order to control for heritability. If we go on carrying out research that only measures biological or psychosocial variables without attempting to combine them, we will remain stuck in a groove of unidimensional thinking.

The BPS model provides a structure to understand personality development. It is not a detailed guideline to measure causality, but a conceptual framework for investigation and assessment. But it is consistent with what we know from research about personality, and particularly about the FFM.

Thus my take home-message is this: since personality is a complex construct that requires a complex theory, reduction to single risk factors is not the answer, and a BPS model can do better. The next two chapters will show how the model can be applied to mental disorders.

Chapter 7

Personality and Mental Disorders

How Personality Underlies Psychopathology

We all have a personality. Yet while some trait profiles are risk factors for developing mental disorders, one need not conclude that evaluating personality in clinical practice means that patients have personality disorders. But even in people who do not meet criteria for PD diagnoses, traits can work for or against them. Personality traits underlie symptoms because they make people more or less sensitive to their environment. That explains why stressors do not affect everyone in the same way

Highly neurotic patients are prone to negative emotions that may not cause trouble in the short term, but that can eventually present clinically as anxiety and depression. As Chapter 8 will discuss, we can use interventions originally designed for PDs to treat neuroticism in patients with common mental disorders (Barlow et al, 2020). For example, therapists can teach their patients skills to regulate emotions when they are too intense, to learn how to tolerate distress, and to slow down before reacting. Patients can also learn how to control impulsivity using some of these same skills and can also avoid being unhelpfully antagonistic.

Widiger and Trull have described several mechanisms that govern the relationship between personality and mental disorders. The first is a *vulnerability/risk* model, in which personality traits directly lead to the development of disorders or enhance the impact of exposure to risk factors. The second is a *pathoplasty* model, in which personality traits affect the course, severity, and treatment response of disorders. The third is a *common cause* model, in which personality traits are predictive of mental disorders because they share genetic and environmental risk factors. The fourth is a spectrum model, in which traits and psychopathology lie on a common dimension that reflects the extremes of personality function. The fifth is a *scar* model, in which episodes of mental disorders modify personality

DOI: 10.4324/9781003519942-7

traits from premorbid levels. These mechanisms are by no means mutually exclusive, and all of them can be involved. This chapter will focus on the closely related common cause and spectrum models.

Personality profiles help to explain why psychotherapies that only target symptoms do not always succeed. For much the same reason, antidepressants are helpful for only about half of the patients for whom they are prescribed (Rush et al, 2019). With this in mid, a personality-based approach to psychopathology can add a valuable perspective to clinical practice. It is too limiting to focus only on symptoms while giving insufficient priority to traits.

Let us now briefly examine the role of personality in some of the mental disorders that most frequently present in clinical practice.

Depression, Anxiety, and Personality

Depression and anxiety are the most common symptomatic presentations in clinical practice and are often present in the same patients. These are the paradigmatic examples of *internalizing disorders*. In other words, their features reflect inner suffering more than the problematic behaviors that are the main feature of *externalizing disorders*.

The distinction between internalizing and externalizing features originated in child psychiatry, but it applies equally to adults (Achenbach et al, 2016). Women usually have more internalizing symptoms, while men tend to have more externalizing behaviors (Hartung and Lefler, 2019). Moreover, patients with anxiety and depression tend to be treatment-seeking. That helps explain why therapists tend to see more women than men. These are real differences, not social constructs. Unless your work focuses on addictions, forensics, or schizophrenia, you will have a preponderance of women in your practice.

The pathology that lies behind depression and anxiety is more complex than it seems. This is reflected in the fact that a significant number of patients do not respond to standard treatments, including both psychotherapy and medication. That can lead to much effort in practice to changing prescriptions. Yet these problems can often be better accounted for by personality traits that interfere with learning more functional patterns of emotion regulation and behavior.

The FFM does not attempt to distinguish between anxiety and depression, which are in any case highly comorbid with each other. Major depression is generally associated with higher neuroticism, lower extraversion, and lower conscientiousness (Alizadeh et al, 2018; Klein et al, 2011). FFM scores in anxiety disorders are characterized by a similar pattern (Watson, 2022). We do know why depression or anxiety predominate in individual patients, but some evidence points to using facets to identify more specific clinical presentations (Rector et al, 2012).

Categorical diagnosis tends to encourage clinicians to see depression as a single pathological process, which it is not. In this way, the *DSM* and ICD systems are misleading. We worry too much about whether patients meet the criteria listed in these manuals. We need to take the diagnosis of "major depression" with a grain of salt. Using such a broad construct conflates many different clinical presentations, leading to a low bar for diagnosis.

These distinctions are not just theoretical. Depression and anxiety vary greatly in severity. Severe depressions may require hospitalization, while mild depressions can be managed in an office practice. Also, severe cases of depression respond better to medication than milder episodes (Parker, 2005). Similarly anxiety can either some make patients house-bound, while others live with their worries,

A unitary view of symptoms leads to a practice of relying too much on antidepressants, which do not work in everyone. Some patients do need a different biological treatment. Others need psychotherapies that go beyond standard CBT.

Research offers strong support for the view that most gains in psychotherapy can be achieved in shorter periods—usually within a few months (Corpas et al, 2021). But that still leaves us with a percentage of the clinical population that has a "treatment resistant depression" (Voisnekos et al, 2020).

Psychiatrists have used a number of biological options for managing treatment resistance. For example, severe depressions can respond to electro-convulsive therapy or neuro-stimulation (Nygren et al, 2023). But depressed patients may not always have a melancholic clinical picture. What is not always considered is that dysfunctional personality traits, as well as diagnosable personality disorders, make biological treatments less than consistently effective (Ormel et al, 2022; Takahashi et al, 2013).

Personality does not have to change radically for depressive symptoms to resolve, even when they have been present for some time. Traits can be modified by teaching skills for managing emotions, curbing impulsivity, making close relationships work, and finding a niche in the world (Paris, 1998; Tyrer and Tyrer, 2018). By and large, symptoms can become less prominent (or even remit entirely) when patients change how they *use* their personality to cope with challenges in life. To understand why this is so, it is important to consider that modified traits yield a better tradeoff between positive and negative effects.

Personality-based treatment is most relevant for milder depressions, but there are also methods that have been shown to be useful in severe cases.

However, depressed patients may go through several rounds of pharmaco-therapy without gaining access to evidence-based psychotherapies. In the absence of therapy, they may not be receiving the best treatment.

Similar principles apply to anxiety disorders (panic disorder, generalized anxiety disorder, and social anxiety disorder). Each of these syndromes are linked to high levels of neuroticism. Chapter 8 will show how disorders with this profile can be managed using a common protocol for treatment.

I will not attempt to apply these ideas to the 300 or so diagnoses listed in the *DSM-5-TR*. However, I need to note that obsessive-compulsive dis-order (OCD) is no longer considered an anxiety disorder, even if patients may be comorbid for one of those categories. OCD is associated with high neuroticism, low extraversion, and low agreeableness, and is not neces-sarily comorbid with obsessive-compulsive personality disorder (Zhang and Takahashi, 2024). OCD is usually been treated with psychotherapy and/or SSRI antidepressants, but has a more problematic response to treat-ment (Castle et al, 2015)

Post-Traumatic Stress Disorder and Personality

The construct of post-traumatic stress disorder (PTSD) is based on an assumption that stressful life events by themselves can cause mental dis-orders. Yet PTSD only occurs in 5–10% of those exposed to trauma, and longitudinal studies show that this disorder to be particularly uncommon in those who have never had a previous psychiatric diagnosis (McNally, 2023). Rates are indeed higher after the most severe traumatic events, such as rape, but PTSD still only affects a minority (about 20%) of such cases. The explanation, once again, lies in trait profiles. People who are high in neuroticism are much more at risk for the disorder. And women who have higher levels of this trait (and who have other internalizing disorders) are more likely than men to develop PTSD (Kofman et al, 2024).

Longitudinal studies of people whose occupation involves exposure to traumatic stressors (police, firefighters) show that even in these groups, most do not develop PTSD, and that high levels of trait neuroticism are a stronger predictor of post-traumatic symptoms.

In other words, the more sensitive you are to your environment, the more likely you will be at risk for post-traumatic symptoms. We must, therefore, question the assumption that PTSD is entirely (or even largely) caused by exposure to trauma. Personality trait profiles marked by high levels of neuroticism are a major risk factor. When PTSD is the outcome, we need to think about gene–environment interactions, in which people with a neurotic temperament react symptomatically to environmental challenges.

Substance Use Disorders and Personality

Substance use describes a group of externalizing disorders associated with behavioral dysregulation that involve misuse of or addiction to drugs. The most frequent presentation in clinical settings is alcohol abuse, which affects about 12% of the general population (Grant et al, 2017).

People who have addictions do not necessarily seek treatment. The majority of cases are seen in males, who are less likely to come to professionals. Also, patients with externalizing disorders, rooted in egosyntonic traits, are more likely to blame circumstances or other people for their problems.

Substance abuse describes a broad domain of disorders: not all users have the same preferences, and not every trait profile should be expected to be the same. But Trull and Sher (1994), later replicated by Fotstad et al (2022), reported that substance use is associated with a broad range of FFM domains, marked by higher neuroticism, lower extraversion, higher openness, lower agreeableness, and lower conscientiousness.

Substance use disorders reflect problems with emotion dysregulation and impulsivity (Jakubczyk et al, 2018). These features are challenging for treatment, and the early steps of engagement may be critical, as shown by research on motivational interviewing (Miller and Rollnick, 2012). Substance use, when continuous over time, reduces longevity, but those who can remain in recovery can do well (Chinneck et al, 2018).

While there is not necessarily a specific "addictive personality", some people with addictions move from one substance to another attempting to manage dysphoric emotions. The heritability of substance use points to a separate genetic pathway that interacts with other traits. But a tendency to crave substances is related to personality traits of impulsivity and Neuroticism. These traits are also higher across behavioral addictions, including gambling (Zilberman et al, 2018). An ability to find substitutes for drugs and alcohol to deal with emotional distress is one of the key factors in recovery from addiction.

Eating Disorders and Personality

This group of mental disorders includes three main types: anorexia nervosa, bulimia nervosa, and binge eating disorder (which can also co-occur). These categories differ in relation to personality trait profiles (Steiger et al, 2023). While patients with eating disorders are usually high in neuroticism, anorexia is associated with perfectionism (i.e., overly high conscientiousness), while bulimia and binge eating are more associated with emotion dysregulation (i.e., neuroticism), as well as with impulsivity, (i.e., low conscientiousness.) Once again, personality seems to be the hidden risk factor that helps explain why people develop one type of disorder or another.

Implications for Practice

Diagnoses of mental disorders may not always lead to the best treatment. These days, while psychopharmacology plays a major role in managing internalizing disorders, almost half of all patients with these symptoms do not respond well to treatment (Kalin, 2020). Instead, as Chapters 8 and 9 will show, considering personality as a major risk factor in this population can guide a trait-based approach to treatment with psychotherapy. While personality profiles are generally stable over time, they can be modified to some extent in patients who develop psychopathology.

Chapter 8

Personality and Personality Disorders

How Personality Traits Shape Personality Disorders

Personality disorders (PDs) describe patterns of emotion, thought, and behavior that are associated with long-term difficulties with a sense of self, interpersonal relationships, and functioning in society. These diagnoses are not always recognized. Doing so requires accepting that they are genuine forms of psychopathology. PD diagnoses require clinical experience, supplemented by tools for personality assessment.

PDs are broad, comorbid, and transdiagnostic. This makes them difficult to separate from other mental disorders. In North America (and elsewhere), clinicians have used the ten PD categories listed in the *DSM-5-TR* manual, unchanged since 1980. The *DSM* groups them into three clusters (A or odd, B or impulsive, and C or anxious), although patients may not fit into any one cluster or category (Zimmerman et al, 2005).

PDs have commonalities in their FFM profiles, and most have high levels of neuroticism, low levels of conscientiousness, and low levels of agreeableness. The impulsive cluster is particularly marked by this profile (Widiger, 2015). The anxious cluster tends to be marked by a different pattern: obsessive-compulsive PD is associated with high conscientiousness (Samuel and Widiger, 2011), avoidant PD with introversion and neuroticism (Lynam et al, 2012), and dependent PD with high agreeableness and neuroticism (Gore and Pincus, 2013).

We are in the midst of a change in the way we diagnose PDs. We need a better way to identify these cases in clinical settings. But experts have not agreed to a consensus about how to proceed. Some want to keep categories but root them in trait profiles, while others want to replace categories with a fully dimensional system.

We need not, however, retain all ten PD categories listed in *DSM-R-TR* (Paris, 2015b). Several (i.e., histrionic, paranoid, schizoid) have little research support. It would also not be a great loss if we were to drop outdated diagnoses such as histrionic personality (based on dramatic

DOI: 10.4324/9781003519942-8

behaviors), or dependent personality (almost entirely based on a single feature). The same can be said for categories such as paranoid and schizoid PDs that can be folded into the category of schizotypal PD, which is probably a sub-clinical variant of psychosis (Rosell et al, 2014).

Moreover, we need a much better way to describe patients who do not fit any category, who can only be considered as having an "unspecified" PD, but who form the largest group of PDs in practice (Zimmerman et al, 2005). That is one of the main reasons many favor a dimensional and quantitative system.

Diagnosing PDs

Personality trait profiles can guide clinicians treating common mental disorders. But when traits seriously affect functioning over the life span, we can (and should) make an additional diagnosis of a PD. When present, the treatment of other symptoms, either with psychopharmacology and psychotherapy) is significantly less successful (French et al, 2017).

As discussed in Chapter 7, a failure to take personality profiles into account may explain why so many patients treated for depression fail to achieve a stable remission. Thus, the picture of "treatment-resistant depression" only tells us whether patients are responding to standard therapies, either psychotherapy or medication. But this scenario may be related either to problematic traits (Takahashi et al. 2013), or to the presence of a diagnosable and comorbid PD (Newton-Howes et al, 2006; Danayan et al, 2024). That requires a shift in perspective from focusing on symptoms to traits that can be targeted and modified using personality-specific methods of therapy.

In many ways, PDs can be understood as pathological amplifications of trait profiles. The most important of these are, once again, high levels of neuroticism. This trait becomes problematic when emotions are both intense and dysregulated. As we have seen, neuroticism lies behind many problems affecting health, as well as a vulnerability to a range of mental disorders.

These relationships could support a dimensional approach to diagnosis, either by focusing on broad domains, as in the FFM or similar methods, for the identification of pathological trait profiles. Even though dimensions may not fully account for all forms of personality pathology, they have real advantages.

For this reason, I support the need for a dimensional model of personality (such as the FFM) that can better account for individual differences, both in patients and nonpatients. But I do not favor a blanket rejection of categorical diagnoses.

Clinicians still need to classify the problems they evaluate and treat. For this reason, diagnosis has played, and still plays, a major role in clinical practice. Diagnostic categories frame symptoms within a broad domain of psychopathology based on similarities in etiology, clinical features, outcome, and treatment response. For example, it has long been crucial to distinguish between schizophrenia and bipolar disorder, since these diagnoses respond differently to pharmacological treatment (Dunner, 1992). Similarly, diagnosing borderline PD guides clinicians to recommend specialized forms of psychotherapy (Paris, 2025).

The problem is that patients meeting criteria for a specific diagnosis can have substantial individual differences. Diagnoses of mental disorders can also be misleading if they do not account for traits or transdiagnostic spectra of psychopathology. The current *DSM* or ICD categories communicate important information but are not diagnoses in the same way as in general medicine. Most are syndromes that lack biological markers to support their validity or specificity. Mental disorders will eventually need to be radically re-classified once their causes are better understood. But at this point, we do not know enough about the brain to develop a truly valid diagnostic system.

Even so, we are so used to current methods of diagnosis that psychiatrists, psychologists, and other mental health professionals feel free to attach firm diagnoses to mental problems. Today, patients are joining the game. They can read about their symptoms on the internet and come to their own conclusions (which they expect us to confirm—even when they are wrong). Both clinicians and patients are tempted to seize on one psychopathological feature without seeing a larger picture. They then generalize from features that are not specific to one disorder but can be associated with multiple diagnoses.

Impressionistic practice can lead to diagnostic epidemics (Frances, 2013). There have been many diagnostic fads in psychiatry, which these days include over-diagnosis of conditions such as bipolar disorders, post-traumatic stress disorder, attention deficit hyperactivity disorder, and autism spectrum disorders (Paris, 2020a). It is particularly tempting to focus on a diagnosis that identifies problems that are believed to be treatable with a single prescription or a specific form of therapy.

While categories are useful in many domains of science, they are provisional in psychiatry and need not be reified. Diagnosis is a tool that can be used all too easily or inappropriately. But trait profiles describe differences between patients who meet criteria for the same categorical diagnosis.

To consider an analogy from the harder sciences, we accept that the physical world is made of particles that are also waves, and of waves that are also particles. A complete description in particle physics requires both.

Another example concerns our understanding of speciation in biology: While each species has unique characteristics, they have evolved gradually over time and may not have precise boundaries. At some point, natural selection prevents interbreeding with other species. But even then, categories have ragged edges, leading to arguments over whether species are truly separate. Like psychological traits, biological variations lie on a continuum, and every individual has a unique profile.

In psychology, these profiles are described by individual differences in personality—traits that can be advantageous or disadvantageous depending on context and circumstance. Thus, we can evaluate commonalities in pathology with diagnosis, leaving adequate room to describe the finer-grained individual differences in trait profiles. This is why personality assessment adds useful information to the process of evaluating patients.

Up to now, there has been more research on categorical diagnoses than on traits. One reason is that the structure of our minds is also categorical. (This bias is sometimes dismissed as "essentialism", but some things are truly essential.) Even so, we need not become unreasonably attached to diagnostic categories but supplement them by conducting personality assessment.

The Alternate Model for Personality Disorder (AMPD)

The *DSM-5*-TR system for diagnosing PDs uses a model that has not changed in 45 years. By and large, diagnoses in a manual should not be revised without strong evidence for doing so (Zimmerman, 2022). That was why, after massive efforts over several years by a workgroup, a proposal to replace the older system with a hybrid and largely dimensional approach in 2013 was not accepted by the American Psychiatric Association. Instead, it was moved to Section III of the *DSM-5* manual (diagnoses requiring more research).

The Alternate Model for Personality Disorders (AMPD) is not yet in the main body of the manual, even though another decade of research has supported and refined its validity. The American Psychiatric Association is currently considering moving it (in a simpler format) to the main part of its manual.

The AMPD classifies PDs according to their trait profiles. Patients need to meet two criteria. Criterion A describes the general features of any PD that affect self and relationships). A wide range of problems with identity and intimacy can be assessed using a *Level of Personality Functioning Scale* (LPFS; or in a briefer form as the LPFS-BF 2.0; Krueger and Hobbs, 2020). This measure yields an overall score indicating the presence of a PD.

Patients who meet Criterion A are then assessed on Criterion B, a profile of pathological trait domains including negative affectivity, detachment, psychoticism, antagonism, and disinhibition. These domains are similar to the FFM (the exception is psychoticism). Another instrument, the *Personality Inventory for DSM-5* (PID-5) can be used to measure these patterns (Krueger and Hobbs, 2020). The cut-off points for each trait must reflect at least moderate abnormality and functional impairment.

These trait profiles can then be used to make one of six categorical diagnoses—schizotypal, antisocial, borderline, narcissistic, obsessive-compulsive, and avoidant PDs. The result is a "hybrid" system that uses traits to build categories. The AMPD has stimulated a large body of research. Up to now, since it is not in the main section of the manual, few clinicians are using it. But there is a recently published book guiding readers to its use (Bach et al, 2024). Diagnoses are rooted in five dysfunctional traits: negative affectivity, detachment, antagonism, disinhibition, and psychoticism. (The current proposal for modifying the AMPD also includes compulsivity as a sixth trait.)

The AMPD was a move forward by developing a hybrid system. It contrasts with the ICD-11, in which BPD is the only category retained on top of dimensional scores. While a BPD diagnosis can be central to planning, its trait profiles offer fine-grained details.

Let us now briefly examine the six categories that the AMPD describes as based on pathological trait profiles. The AMPD system describes six categories of PD instead of 10. I will have the most to say about BPD, which has been studied in hundreds of research papers.

Borderline Personality Disorder

Diagnosis

The most researched PD category is BPD. Its main features are instability of self-image, interpersonal relationships, and affects, accompanied by impulsivity, risk taking, and/or hostility. It also has features that go beyond trait variations, particularly when related to chronic suicidality. The diagnosis has both externalizing and internalizing features, and its effect on psychosocial functioning is more like a major mental disorder.

BPD has a very large empirical literature (Paris, 2020a). That helps explain why, in spite of much controversy, the diagnosis has been retained in most classifications, even in the ICD-11, which had originally aimed to remove all categories of PD diagnosis.

BPD is common, and has a community prevalence of 2% (Trull et al, 2010) and can be diagnosed in up to 10% of patients with PDs who present to clinics (Zimmerman et al, 2005).

The reason why BPD is the most heavily researched PD is that patients with this diagnosis are difficult to manage. They often come to emergency settings, and most will either have had suicidal ideation or have made suicide attempts. About 7–10% will eventually die by suicide (Paris, 2020a).

Let me now summarize what I have written elsewhere about this disorder (Paris, 2020a, 2025).

The FFM profile in BPD is high neuroticism (anxiousness, angry hostility, depressiveness, impulsiveness, and vulnerability), high extraversion (openness to fantasy and excitement-seeking), low agreeableness, low conscientiousness, that is, impulsivity, as well as high openness (Widiger and McCabe, 2020). Thus, in line with its clinical complexity and extensive comorbidity, BPD is associated with abnormalities on all five factors. Nonetheless, *emotion dysregulation* remains its central feature (Crowell et al, 2009; Linehan, 1993).

Drilling down, BPD patients can have relatively high levels of neuroticism in all its facets (Trull and Brown, 2013). These patients are thin-skinned, and when things go wrong in relationships, or are perceived that way, emotions can be highly unstable. Unlike patients with bipolar disorder, mood can change by the hour—not by the week or the month. Interactions with other people may easily be seen as invalidating, and relationships suffer from intense needs for support combined with strong negative emotions.

BPD is also marked by high impulsivity and low conscientiousness. The range of impulsive behaviors in these patients is quite broad, marked by suicidality (threats, attempts, or chronic ideation), self-harm (particularly cutting), as well as substance use and eating disorders.

BPD is associated with low levels of agreeableness (Trull and Brown, 2013). Antagonism is the trait that most interferes with therapy.

In summary, at least three of the five factors in BPD fall within a pathological spectrum. Some aspects of the disorder, however, go beyond FFM descriptions. About half of BPD patients have "micro-psychotic" symptoms such as dissociation and/or auditory hallucinations in response to stress (Minarikova et al, 2022). This feature may reflect high openness but is better seen as the "borderline" with psychosis that gave its name to the disorder.

Since BPD presents a complex clinical picture, clinicians may be impressed by its "comorbidities" such as depression, anxiety, and substance use. But research has shown that problems in all domains of BPD tend to hang together. In fact, some studies of the traits behind the disorder show that it most closely links with a "p factor", that is, a general measure of psychological impairment (Gluschkoff et al, 2021).

Life Course of BPD Patients

Unlike neurodevelopmental disorders, BPD is rarely diagnosed in child-hood, although some studies have observed its features prior to puberty (Belsky et al, 2012; Guzder et al, 1996). The disorder usually begins in adolescence and peaks in youth (Paris, 2020). Many clinicians are reluc-tant to make a BPD diagnosis before age 18, but *DSM-5*-TR states that PDs can be identified at earlier ages if symptoms have continued for more than a year. As pointed out by Boone et al (2025), PDs are missed because of a preference for diagnoses of symptomatic disorders, and due to the incorrect view of clinicians that adolescence is normally a time of severe stress,

Self-harm (nonsuicidal self-injury, NSSI) is a frequent feature of ado-lescent BPD, but only a minority of adolescents cut themselves for years (Moran et al, 2012). A follow-up study by our group found that those who also have more severe emotion dysregulation are most at risk (Biskin et al, 2021). Thus, NSSI does not, by itself, predict BPD; this behavior tends to spread through social contagion (Paris, 2024).

The good news is that BPD tends to remit with time, sometimes early in its course, and symptoms decline in the majority of cases by age 35–40. This may be due to brain maturation, in which traits of neuroticism and impulsivity become less intense with maturity. It could also be due to a process of learning to avoid situations in life that trigger symptoms.

In a retrospective 27-year follow-up study of BPD patients, our group found very few who still met diagnostic criteria at age 50 (Paris et al, 2001). This cohort had been evaluated at a general hospital, and most had been briefly admitted for suicidality, but we found much less chronicity at follow-up. The majority of patients were working, although only about half had either a stable partner or children.

Prospective studies have found similar results. Gunderson et al (2011), in a 10-year follow-up of patients from multiple sites, reported that most patients go into in remission. Zanarini (2019), in a 24-year prospective follow-up of patients admitted to a psychiatric hospital, also reported that most cases went into remission, but that those who continued using substances were more likely ending up unemployed and on disability (Zanarini et al, 2024). We can conclude that the prognosis of BPD is good but variable.

Suicide rates in follow-up studies of BPD patients fall somewhere between 5% and 10% (Paris, 2020c). Our research group found a rate of 10%, but one the mean age at suicide was 37. BPD patients are most at risk when their lives fail to straighten out, and when treatment has been unsuccessful. On the other hand, younger patients who attempt suicide and are seen at ERs are much less likely to die by suicide at that stage, and we can worry about them a little less. But another 10% of our patients died young from medical illnesses, a finding later confirmed by Fok et al (2012).

Does Childhood Adversity Cause BPD?

Adverse events in childhood take many forms, but surveys around the world confirm that they increase the overall risk for adult psychopathology (McLaughlin et al, 2010). Yet we need to assess the size of these effects, and to find out to what extent they are mediated by other risk factors.

For example, parental loss is a major stressor for children, but research on its long-term effects shows that the circumstances following a death are more important than the loss itself (Luecken and Roubinov, 2012). Similarly, while research on the long-term effects of divorce shows an increased risk for psychopathology in adulthood, the circumstances around family breakdown are much more important (Amato and Booth, 1997).

The most researched area of childhood adversity is abuse and neglect, and a large body of research has assessed their long-term effects. But the term "abuse" needs to be carefully defined. Mistreatment of children is an emotional issue, and this concept can itself be abused. For example, *childhood sexual abuse* (CSA) should be limited to sexual activity carried out by adults with children, and to acts that involve physical contact (Fergusson, 1999). Even using this narrower definition, we should exclude events that are formally illegal, but not abusive, such as sexual relations between a 16-year old girl and an 18-year old boy.

There is a vast body of research on CSA. It is a risk factor for a wide range of adult mental disorders, but does not, by itself, consistently predict them. Long-term outcome depends on the nature of the abuse, as defined by parameters (Fergusson, 1999). The relationship of the victim to the perpetrator is the most crucial; others relate to severity, that is, the nature of the sexual act, and its duration. Thus, a single incident of molestation by a nonfamily member during childhood is unlikely to cause or account for an adult mental disorder. In contrast, father–daughter incest, which is usually experienced as a profound betrayal, has more severe long-term consequences.

Another issue that emerges from research on CSA is that while this risk factor has an independent effect on adult psychopathology, outcomes can often be accounted for the family dysfunction accompanying abuse (Fergusson et al, 2011). Thus, children from dysfunctional families are more likely to be abused, and to lack support from their family when abuse happens. This point is not always understood by clinicians. Even when a history of CSA is elicited, one cannot explain current symptoms exclusively on that basis. We need not oversimplify the complex pathways to disorders.

Physical abuse (PA) in childhood has been less extensively researched. The term should only be used when abuse occurs inside a family, not for bullying by peers. Research on PA is less common but yields similar findings to CSA (Malinovsky-Rummell and Hansen, 1993). It is a risk factor for the development of mental disorders, but outcomes depend on severity and circumstance (as with CSA, many effects of PA can be attributed to family dysfunction; Fergusson et al, 2011).

The term *emotional abuse* (EA) refers to demeaning and hurtful comments from parents about children and is one of the variables measured in a widely used interview for child abuse (Fink et al, 1995). While not thoroughly researched, EA may also be a risk factor for adult mental disorders (Finzi-Dottan and Karu, 2006), and it is very frequently reported by BPD patients (Zanarini, 2000).

Neglect can refer to either physical neglect (failure to provide minimal care in the protection of children), or to the more subtle risk factor of emotional neglect (failure of parents to approve of and/or provide emotional support). Emotional neglect has been widely studied as a risk factor for mental disorders. But it can be difficult to measure, given the limitations of self-report (Hernandez et al, 2012).

Clinicians need to keep in mind the principle that *family dysfunction* underlies all forms of abuse and neglect. Families with high levels of conflict and low levels of positive interaction are more likely to mistreat and/or fail to respond appropriately to children.

Resilience is a key concept for understanding the outcome of childhood adversity. The majority of children who suffer single adversities do not grow up to develop mental disorders, but become normal adults (Rutter, 2012). However multiple adversities, and a temperamental vulnerability to adversity, carries a much higher risk (Rutter, 2007). Thus, the mechanisms behind resilience are partly genetic, partly environmental, and mainly reflect gene-environment interactions. For example, children with positive personality traits can find alternative attachment figures to buffer the effect of adversities, but children who are more sensitive, neurotic, and introverted, have a difficult time doing so (Rutter, 2012).

Since resilience is ubiquitous, one cannot assume that mental disorders will be caused by single adversities, or that specific adversities will predictably lead to a mental disorder. For each type, adversities increase the risk, but do not directly lead to disorders. By and large, even the most traumatic events do not lead to illness unless there are multiple risk factors with cumulative effects, or a "double hit" in which a vulnerable temperament produces gene-environment interactions (Rutter, 2007).

While these principles are well known to researchers, they are not always understood by clinicians. Unique causes do not usually produce unique effects. Even in medicine, univariate models do not often explain illness, and multivariate models are usually required. Cicchetti and Rogosch (1996) described the complexity of pathways in developmental psycho-pathology as reflecting both *equifinality* (different risk factors leading to the same outcome), and *multifinality* (the same risk factors leading to different outcomes).

In spite of these complexities, clinical assessment of patients can include an exploration of childhood adversity. This information can almost always be elicited by tactful questioning. It is easier to obtain if one spends less time on symptom checklists, and more on life history. Whether or not adversity is directly or indirectly related to current symptoms, knowing about early experience helps therapists to understand their patients.

Adult BPD patients report a particularly high frequency of childhood adversity. This relationship has been consistently found in retrospective studies (Zanarini, 2000) and can be readily confirmed by interviewing family members (Laporte and Guttman, 1996). These relationships have been further supported by longitudinal studies of children in the community (e.g., Johnson et al, 1999) which show a significant relationship between adversity and BPD symptoms. These outcomes have also been confirmed by long-term follow-up of children who had been involved in the judicial system because they were abused (Widom et al, 2009).

When these findings first became widely known, about 25 years ago, some clinicians concluded that abuse and neglect are the main *cause* of BPD. This idea is still widely held but it is mistaken. For example, the claim that CSA fulfills criteria for causality established in medicine (Ball and Links, 2009) is incorrect, given that it is only one risk factor among many, and since it intercorrelates with many other risks (Fergusson et al, 1999). Also, BPD is not a form of post-traumatic stress disorder (Lewis and Grenyer, 2009), nor is it, as often claimed, "complex PTSD" (Herman and van der Kolk, 1987). That diagnosis is listed in the ICD-11, but in *DSM-5-TR*. Not all BPD patients experience childhood adversity, and some events that have been scored by researchers as examples of CSA are not that traumatic (Paris et al, 1994a, 1994b). Thus, BPD demonstrates multifinality, and child abuse is an example of equifinality.

It is also not true that patients with BPD who lack histories of abuse must have forgotten or "repressed" these experiences (McNally, 2003). While supporters of traumatic causation of BPD have made this claim, it is not consistent with a large body of research on human memory (McNally, 2003).

Another complication involves determining the precise frequency of child abuse in BPD patients. These numbers depend on how abuse is defined. Our own research (Paris et al, 1994a, 1994b), in a sample large enough to conduct multivariate analyses, supported the findings of community studies showing that CSA is most likely to be a risk factor when a caretaker is involved, and when incidents are severe and multiple. Our study, as well as that of Zanarini (2000), and later confirmed by Laporte et al (2013), found that about 25% of BPD patients have been sexually abused by a caretaker (often a step-parent). We also found that while about a third of all BPD patients reported long-term CSA, that another third only reported single events (almost always molestation by a non-family member), and that another third reported no abuse at all. These conclusions have been supported by meta-analyses which failed to show that child abuse is a strong risk factor (Fossati et al, 1999; Porter et al, 2020).

CSA is, however, associated with more severe symptoms of BPD and slower rate of recovery.

In summary, CSA is an important risk factor for BPD, but has more impact when it occurs within a family, when it lasts for years, and when the form of sexual acts are more damaging (Paris, 2017).

Since physical abuse is more common in boys, we conducted a study of men with BPD (Paris et al, 1994b). But what we found was a relationship between BPD and CSA, and not between BPD and PA. There is a relationship in women between emotional abuse and BPD (Laporte et al, 2013). However, this adversity, like CSA and PA, is best seen as a marker for broader family dysfunction.

As for emotional neglect, many studies have found this adversity reported by BPD patients more frequently than by patients with other PDs (Zanarini, 2000) or common mental disorders. Linehan (1993) has suggested that children at risk for BPD have an abnormal temperament and need more support to manage emotional dysregulation. It is possible that emotional neglect, a less dramatic and more subtle adversity than CSA or PA, is a risk factor in the large number of patients who have not been abused, or in those who report only single episodes.

Some researchers have proposed that CSA is related to specific symptoms of dissociation or self-harm (Herman and van der Kolk, 1987). Our research group examined this question and found that these phenomena were related to having a diagnosis of BPD, but not to trauma . Thus, symptoms were as common in patients without abuse and those who had been abused. In a meta-analysis of community studies, Klonsky and Meyer (2008) found no direct relationship between CSA and self-harm. A failure to conduct multivariate studies has created an incorrect impression.

There is a need for prospective research on childhood adversities to determine what relation they have to BPD as an outcome. One of the longer study of this kind is the Children in the Community Study (Cohen et al, 2005), which has followed its cohort for several decades. While the results suggested that child abuse is related to symptoms in adulthood, there were not enough clinical cases in this cohort (Johnson et al, 1999).

In recent years, several research groups have followed cohorts at risk longitudinally from childhood to examine these relationships. However, since BPD is rare before puberty, researchers have had to measure features of the disorder rather than identify formal diagnoses. One cohort (Bornovalova et al, 2009) consisted of twin pairs, allowing the researchers to control for temperamental effects. Four other studies include: (1) a birth cohort in the UK, representative of the general population (Belsky et al, 2012), that has followed children up to age 12; (2) a cohort of girls in England and the USA, but in which follow-up was only funded up to age 11; (3) a cohort of girls growing up in a large city (Hipwell et al, 2010) followed to age 10–13. All these studies point to a consistent relationship between early adversity and BPD-like symptoms prior to puberty.

Another approach involves research on children who show clinical features that resemble adult BPD. Along with other research groups, we conducted this kind of study, and showed that adverse experiences in this population were similar to those found in adult cases (Guzder et al, 1996). However, when we followed up these patients, who were mostly boys, into adolescence, they developed general features of PDs, but not BPD.

What can clinicians conclude from this research? About half of BPD patients can be expected to report a serious child adversity of some kind. Clearly abuse and neglect are major risk factors for this disorder. Also, the other half of patients, who do not report serious abuse and neglect, will not necessarily have experienced adequate parenting. Parents who are "good enough" for the average child may not be good enough for those who are vulnerable to the disorder.

The main reason why the post-traumatic theory of BPD is misleading is that it does not apply a stress-diathesis model, failing to take into account interactions between temperament and experience. While childhood trauma is a risk factor for BPD, adverse experiences have a different impact on different children, depending on their personality traits.

Gene–Environment Interactions in BPD

This brings us back to the crucial role of gene–environment interactions (Carpenter et al, 2013). It has also been shown that many of the environmental risk factors in BPD have a strong genetic component due to risky choices that patients make (Distel et al, 2011). Another mechanism concerns genetic differences in sensitivity to environmental adversities, as reflected in personality trait profiles.

Our research group conducted a study in which we compared 56 female probands diagnosed with BPD to their biological sisters (Laporte et al, 2011). We found that only three of the sisters also had BPD, and that none of the others had serious current psychopathology. When we designed the study, we had anticipated we would find that BPD patients would have suffered more trauma, and that sisters free of mental disorder would have suffered less. But that is not what we found. Both probands and sisters described similar experiences in childhood, with only a few measures of severity higher in those with BPD. The most important difference was in personality. BPD patients had an abnormal personality trait profile, with elevations on almost every scale. The most likely explanation is that those who developed the disorder processed traumatic experience in a different way, creating negative feedback loops that lead to serious psychopathology.

Behavior genetic studies show that at least 40% of variance in outcome in BPD is due to heritable influences (Torgersen et al, 2000). That still leaves another half of the variance related to the environment. However, the environmental factors in BPD, as is the case for most mental disorders, are "unshared", that is, siblings brought up by same parents do not share the risk. While one can look outside the family for social risk factors (Millon, 1993), the most useful concept derives from the interactions between temperament and adversity.

Behavior genetics also sheds light on the relationship between trauma and BPD. The longitudinal twin study of children followed into adolescence by Bornovalova and colleagues found an association between childhood abuse and BPD traits stemmed from common genetic factors that overlapped with a vulnerability to both internalizing and externalizing disorders.

The mechanisms behind a temperamental predisposition to BPD are not well understood. They could parallel the mixture of internalizing symptoms (associated with emotion dysregulation) and externalizing symptoms (associated with impulsive behaviors) seen in adult patients (Crowell et al, 2009). Children with such characteristics are more prone to be distressed, to remain distressed, and to act impulsively when distressed (Paris, 2008). They are more sensitive to adverse events, are affected by them more deeply, and react in ways that can make their situation worse. However, there is also evidence that temperamental risks for mental disorders are based on a broader concept of sensitivity to both positive and negative aspects of the environment (Ellis and Boyce, 2008).

Interactions between temperament and life adversities have a broad significance for abnormal psychology. Almost all mental disorders have a genetic component rooted in temperament—even those considered as environmental, such as post-traumatic stress disorder (True et al, 1993).

It is difficult to think multivariately. On the one hand, biological reductionism in contemporary psychiatry has led to a downgrading or dismissal of the psychosocial factors that are so important in shaping mental disorders, and to an over-reliance on inconsistently effective biological interventions (Bracken et al, 2012). On the other hand, traditional views about the primacy of early experience and childhood adversity for psychopathology have sometimes been used to support rather ineffective forms of psychotherapy (Paris, 2000). These models have not been well supported by evidence, and the treatments based on them can do harm. BPD patients can be suggestible and vulnerable to therapeutic methods that encourage false memories. Moreover, current psychopathology drives perceptions of the past (McNally, 2003). Thus, clinical practice in BPD, like the patients themselves, has had a tendency to go to extremes.

Treatment of BPD

It is now well established that most patients with BPD benefit from structured psychotherapies specifically developed for the disorder. But few of these methods promote a strong focus on childhood adversity. While it is always important to validate childhood experiences, effective treatments such as dialectical behavior therapy (Linehan, 1993), mentalization-based treatment (Bateman and Fonagy, 2004), or Systems Training for Emotional Predictability and Problem Solving (Blum et al, 2008) apply cognitive models that focus on current problems, particularly the management of emotion dysregulation, the reduction of impulsivity, and an ability to understand interpersonal encounters.

The origins of BPD are as complex as its clinical features and are best accounted for gene-environment interactions (Paris, 2020a). BPD has a heritable component that accounts for nearly half of its variance. Brain scans suggest that BPD is related to a failure of cortical control of subcortical systems that drive emotional dysregulation (Marceau et al, 2018). While a history of childhood trauma is common, severe trauma (sexual and/or physical abuse) is only seen in about a third of cases (Paris, 2020a).

Thus, trauma is an additional risk factor for BPD rather than a main cause (Winsper, 2018). That why I am not keen about the new diagnosis of "complex PTSD" in ICD-11, which describes many features of BPD and attributes most of them to childhood trauma.

There is some evidence that the prevalence of BPD may have increased due to social risk factors (Paris, 2020b). There is reason to believe that adolescence has become more stressful, as shown by the recent social epidemic of self-harm among teenage girls (Paris, 2024).

In summary, BPD is complex and multidimensional. Even though high neuroticism is a central problem, it does not capture all its features. And while a mix of high neuroticism, low conscientiousness, and low agreeableness is notable, this trait profile is not specific to the disorder.

The AMPD system could help to address the complexity of BPD. This model has now been studied in many research papers and has the support of those who favor trait-based models (e.g., the current editors of the *Journal of Personality Disorders*, Robert Krueger and John Oldham). The AMPD may now be ready to be formally adopted in DSM, either in the 6th edition or sooner (with a proposal for doing so currently under review).

The AMPD profile of BPD can be easily translated into its clinical features, which are about the same in *DSM-5-TR* and ICD-11 (Mulay et al, 2019). However, BPD, by its breadth as a construct, resists being described entirely by dimensions. In this respect, it stands somewhat outside the realm of other PDs, having a resemblance to the more severe disorders in the manual. For that very reason, it is the most problematic PD category for clinicians.

As the next chapter will show, the prognosis of BPD has improved since the development of methods to teach skills in emotion regulation (Linehan, 1993). It has not been shown, however, that whether BPD is diagnosed as a category or as a set of dimensions makes a difference in the outcome of treatment. As will be discussed in Chapter 9, the best data on treatment shows that psychotherapy is effective but does not show any one evidence-based method to be superior.

Antisocial PD

The profile of antisocial PD (ASPD) has features of forensic importance, but these patients are rarely seen in a general mental health practice. The clinical picture in the DSM-5-TR is one of law-breaking, deceit, impulsivity, aggressiveness, disregard for safety, irresponsibility, and lack of remorse (Black, 2022). Antisocial individuals tend to be high in Antagonism but low in Neuroticism (they rarely feel guilty).

The construct of *psychopathy* represents a severe form of antisociality (Hare, 2020). It can be evaluated using the Psychopathy Check List Revised. Psychopathy has also been the subject of a book applying a biopsychosocial model. In a metanalysis that examined both categories, psychopathy and antisocial PD were negatively associated with conscientiousness, but psychopathy had stronger associations with Antagonism. Thus, while not all people with antisocial PD ever go to jail, people with psychopathy are likely to have a criminal record (Hare, 2020).

Based on research findings, *DSM-5-TR* requires that the features of ASPD appear early in childhood as a severe form of conduct disorder, usually associated with callous emotional traits. Adolescents without a past history of conduct disorder may join a gang, but most will stop antisocial behaviors by age 18. When early-onset conduct disorder continues into young adulthood, the diagnosis shifts to ASPD (Moffitt, 2017).

Given the broad definition of ASPD in DSM manuals, this disorder is common in the community—affecting 3% of the population, with a large predominance of males (Moran, 1999). While we see few of these patients in clinical settings, they are more likely to be assessed in prisons and addiction centers. An exception occurs when they are referred by lawyers looking to defend them from a criminal charge. People with ASPD consider their problems as "egosyntonic", due to other people and not themselves (Black, 2022).

Narcissistic PD

Narcissistic PD (NPD) has not been widely researched, and it remains controversial. But there is a large literature on narcissistic traits. People with this profile are characterized by grandiosity, entitlement, exploitative relationships, a lack of empathy, and a need to be admired. The definition of NPD in *DSM-5-TR* focuses on grandiosity, a variable and vulnerable self-esteem, with attempts at regulation through attention and approval seeking, and either overt or covert grandiosity. Like those with ASPD, patients with NPD do not necessarily seek help, partly because they lack self-criticism, and partly out of fear that going to a therapist is a sign of weakness.

The profile of NPD is one of high antagonism, low neuroticism, and high extraversion. Grandiose narcissism correlates with antagonism, as well as traits related to extraversion such as dominance and reward seeking. This trait profile differs somewhat if one accepts a distinction between what has been called grandiose vs. vulnerable narcissism. Bui I am not convinced that a vulnerable type is a variant of the same psychopathology. At this point, vulnerable narcissism is not in any diagnostic manual, and may reflect concept creep. This category is more related to neuroticism: grandiose fantasies without the typical behaviors found in people with NPD (Miller et al, 2018).

There are also people who can be described as having traits within a "dark triad" of psychopathy, narcissism and Machiavellianism (Jones and Paulhus, 2014). That picture is most likely a variant of psychopathy.

There are self-report measures that assess narcissism: the Narcissistic Personality Inventory and the Pathological Narcissism Inventory (Maxwell et al, 2011). One metanalysis found that narcissism of all kinds declines with age (Orth et al, 2024), but not always rapidly or sufficiently to avoid consequences in work and relationships.

We lack a consistently effective treatment for any form of NPD, and there have been thus far no clinical trials for the treatment of the disorder, but only case reports. How could it be otherwise when these patients are highly antagonistic and think they know better than any of the experts?

Avoidant PD

Avoidant PD (AVPD) is described in DSM-5-TR as an avoidance of social situations and inhibition in interpersonal relationships related to feelings of ineptitude and inadequacy, anxious preoccupation with negative evaluation and rejection, and fears of ridicule or embarrassment. The FFM trait profile is one of introversion, low openness to experience, low agreeableness, and low conscientiousness (Lynam et al, 2012). AVPD is common in the community but is less often seen in practice (Reich and Schatzberg, 2021; Weinbrecht et al, 2016), probably because these patients avoid stressful situations.

AVPD overlaps with social anxiety disorder, but it is more severe and pervasive. Its characteristics are social anxiety and inhibition, feelings of inadequacy and inferiority, and social withdrawal. There is a paucity of research on this disorder. But we sometimes see this picture as a long-term outcome of other PDs, in which a patient has shifted, after many disappointments, from a pattern of impulsivity to a more avoidant pattern (Paris, 2025).

Obsessive-Compulsive PD

Obsessive-compulsive PD (OCPD) is characterized by difficulties in establishing and sustaining close relationships, associated with rigid perfectionism, inflexibility, and restricted emotional expression. Its trait profile is dominated by high conscientiousness and high neuroticism (Samuel and Widiger, 2011). It may be one of the easiest disorders to describe using trait dimensions.

People with this trait may not even consider perfectionism to be a problem and wonder how others can be satisfied with imperfect choices in life. When OCPD patients come for therapy, it is most likely to be due to depression brought on when they cannot reach overly high standards for themselves (Hong and Tan, 2021).

This clinical picture is not the same as obsessive-compulsive disorder (OCD), although there can be some overlap. OCPD describes people with standards about self and others that are so high that they interfere with social functioning and may lead to depression when unrealistic expectations are not fulfilled.

Schizotypal PD

Schizotypal PD is described by DSM by impairments in the capacity for social and close relationships, and eccentricities in cognition, perception, and behavior that are associated with distorted self-image and incoherent personal goals and accompanied by suspiciousness and restricted emotional expression. Its FFM profile is characterized by high neuroticism, low extraversion, low agreeableness, as well as high levels of openness sometimes associated with mild forms of thought disorder (Chmielewski et al, 2014). On the basis of family studies, this disorder is considered to be a milder form of schizophrenia, and is cross-categorized as such in *DSM-5-TR*. In the AMPD, it has been now combined with the older but less severe category of schizoid PD. These patients are not help-seeking and are rarely seen in clinics.

PDs in ICD-11

The ICD-11 system for PDs was aimed to be a purely dimensional system. It was developed by a prominent British psychiatrist, Peter Tyrer, long known as a critic of categorical diagnosis for PDs (Tyrer et al, 2019). The story of why BPD, with its broad range of symptoms, was not dropped from diagnostic manuals, as some researchers (Tyrer et al, 2019) thought it should be, is instructive. When this change was proposed, a group of researchers from Europe and the US wrote an article arguing for the retention of BPD (Herpertz et al, 2017). This pushback from researchers who had spent most of their careers studying BPD led to an independent review that eventually allowed for including a "borderline pattern" that closely resembles the description of BPD in DSM-5-TR (Simonsen and Paris, 2025). But all other PDs have been replaced by trait profiles.

There are now books offering guidelines for clinicians in applying the AMPD system (Bach and Simonsen, 2024; Tyrer and Mulder, 2022). Its trait domains are negative affectivity, dissociality, anankastia (compulsivity), negative affectivity, detachment, and disinhibition. They are rather similar to the AMPD and resemble four of the FFM domains. They are measured by a different instrument, the Personality Assessment Questionnaire for ICD-11 (PAQ-11; Clark et al, 2021). Severity is then rated on a five-point scale (no impairment, personality difficulty, mild PD, moderate PD, and severe PD). This is a simpler procedure than the one in the AMPD. But as the system is much newer, it is just beginning to be researched.

Widiger and McCabe (2020) note that both the AMPD and the ICD-11 systems can readily be translated into similar trait domains in the FFM. Both the ICD and the DSM might have used the FFM's trait profiles to describe personality dimensionally. As Widiger and Smith (2025, p.169) point out, both these systems have problems:

> For the DSM-5 AMPD trait model, these include problematic place-ments, inadequate coverage, perceived complexity, and lack of cutoff points. For the DSM-5 AMPD Level of Personality Functioning (LPF), they include the complexity, the questionable presumption that the LPF defines the core of personality disorder, the presumption that the LPF identifies what is unique to the personality disorders, and the premise that the LPF is distinct from the maladaptive traits. Limitations and challenges of the ICD-11 model are the absence of lower-order facet scales and the fact that only the level of severity is required.

I have also wondered why the FFM was not included in *DSM-5* or ICD-11, instead of starting from scratch with new systems. But the manuals were written to encourage simplicity of use for clinicians. As we have seen, the FFM system, though widely used in research, it is less often applied in clinical practice. Yet it accounts for much of the variance in clinical populations with PDs. Its greatest strength is that it has generated thousands of research papers, supporting its validity in both community and clinical settings across the globe.

Living in Two Worlds: Categorical and Dimensional Diagnosis

Diagnosis in medicine has always relied on categories to classify illness. It includes a few dimensional measures (blood pressure and staging of cancers). However, in psychiatry, unlike the rest of medicine, the validity of existing categories is not supported by biomarkers to ground clinical phenomena in endophenotypes. In fact, the biological correlates of mental disorders are almost entirely unknown. For this reason, systems of classification in psychiatry have had to depend on clinical phenomenology rather than on underlying mechanisms of psychopathology. Thus, the current categories in the *DSM-5-TR* system are syndromes, not illnesses with a specific etiology and pathogenesis.

Dimensional measures of psychopathology imply that one need not search for features that would support categories: points of rarity between traits, subclinical phenomena, and disorders, but that observe a smooth progression from normality to pathology that forms a spectrum. In principle, the symptoms of *any* mental disorder could be scored dimensionally. But continuous measures in medicine, such as blood pressure, can still be subject to categorical cut-offs. Also, clinical decision-making in mental health practice has long been a dichotomous procedure, with treatment decisions based on the presence or absence of a categorically defined disorder. One argument in favor of categories is that they separate severe dysfunction from normal variants. Moreover, some categories of PD, especially BPD, have features, such as suicidality, that are not fully accounted for by trait dimensions.

Mental disorders seem to be easier to recognize if one has in mind a characteristic clinical picture, rather than a set of scores. While not every patient will fit these *prototypes*, remembering a set of familiar criteria may be less taxing. It is what clinicians are used to, and they need additional training to replace diagnostic categories with dimensional models. Finally, psychiatry would have to decide at some point whether to convert all diagnoses into dimensions, which would be a radical break from other domains of medicine.

Even so, there are good reasons for using dimensions to describe PDs ion more detail. One is that is usually better in science to describe quantitative data rather than qualitative reports. Another is that the currently influential neuroscience model of psychiatry, in which mental disorders are viewed as brain disorders, has found stronger correlations with neurobiological endophenotypes than with categories. But while PDs have sometimes been considered as "poster children" for a dimensional approach, there are no biomarkers for personality traits—these relationships remain to be discovered.

Here is my summary of the usefulness of the FFM and similar dimensional systems in understanding PDs.

Advantages:

1 Dimensional models solve some of the problems of overlapping criteria that make PD diagnosis unreliable, while profiles tend to be more reliable.
2 Dimensions provide more detailed information about functioning and are closer to what we can observe in practice.
3 Dimensions based on self-report data help providers to overcome clinical biases

Limitations:

1 Dimensions can be nonspecific—just about every patient we see is high in neuroticism.

2 The use of facets has not thus far resolved that problem.
3 We lack biological markers for traits, which are linked to a very large number of alleles in the genome. For this reason, we are tied to data that may not tell us about etiology.

Using Trait Dimensions to Guide Therapy for PDs

This book has focused on how understanding personality structures can help therapists manage a wide variety of patients. There is one example in the domain of PDs that shows that doing so is possible.

This is the development of dialectical behavior therapy (DBT; Linehan, 1993), a breakthrough in the history of clinical psychology. Moreover, DBT is based on a biopsychosocial model, and synthesizes many points of view. It contrasts with narrower ideas that attempt to explain every problem as due to adverse events early in life. It will be discussed in more detail in the next chapter.

We have come a long way in research on PDs over my lifetime. Many if not most patients with BPD seek help, and evidence shows that therapy is often successful (Storebø et al, 2020). But we need methods to treat a wider range of personality psychopathology. The problem is that research on most of the other PDs, whether diagnosed using dimensions or categories, is either not available or not encouraging. For example, patients with avoidant PD suffer greatly but often fail to do well in treatment; Weinbrecht et al (2016) rightly describe this disorder as "neglected". But we lack convincing evidence from clinical trials that therapy for these patients is effective. Much the same can said for the treatment of narcissistic PD, for which there is also little evidence for efficacy of psychotherapy.

The next chapter will examine the extent to which we could increase access to evidence-based treatments for a wider range of patients.

Chapter 9

Personality and Psychotherapy

Traits and Psychotherapy

Personality trait profiles predict many outcomes in life, including success in work and stability in relationships. These are among the core features of a personality disorder (PD). This chapter will focus on treating patients with these diagnoses.

Personality also has an important relationship to the success of psychological treatment. It has long been known that the higher the level of functioning in patients, the more likely they are to benefit from psychotherapy. This is not just a case of the rich getting richer and the poor getting poorer, but is a marker for resilience.

People can be high in problematic traits but find ways to work around them. That is, until something happens that they cannot manage, leading to clinically apparent distress. But psychological treatment is not just about symptoms. It needs to teach patients how to *work* with traits to attain a better level of functioning.

The main target of treatment for PDs is usually high levels of neuroticism. Engaging in psychotherapy also requires some degree of conscientiousness and agreeableness.

Conscientiousness is a basic requirement for good results in therapy. Patients need to show up regularly for appointments. (Dropouts are all too common in practice, particularly when treating people with impulsive trait patterns.) Moreover, patients must be prepared to face the most difficult problems with their personality and to commit themselves to change. Resistance to that level of change is usually an issue, and therapists need to be active in challenging current behavioral patterns. We need to show patients that these behaviors are just not working for them, and that waiting for other people to change is a bad strategy. This approach requires a good amount of tact—a key focus of training in psychotherapy. The methods of Motivational Interviewing (Miller and Rollnick, 2012), gradually guiding patients toward change, can be used to get these messages across.

DOI: 10.4324/9781003519942-9

With these principles in mind, there is another reason why understanding personality is as important as targeting symptoms. Personality-informed therapy requires skills in empathy and imagination. When the patient and the therapist are on the same page, this is an effective way of providing mental health treatment.

Moreover, what can be called *personality-informed psychotherapy* is more holistic, in that it focuses on the person who has the symptoms. It contrasts with methods such as "trauma-informed psychotherapy" which focuses on symptoms and risks seeing patients as victims (McNally, 2023). This approach to treatment views psychopathology in the context of the life course and in differences in the way people cope with their environment. It focuses on present functioning, as opposed to events in the distant past.

What Research Tells Us about Psychotherapy

Research supporting the efficacy of psychotherapy is voluminous. I direct the reader to several books that offer up-to-date summaries of what empirical studies have found (Wampold, 2019). Here I will briefly summarize what is known—

1 Psychotherapy works for a broad variety of patients, both for relief of symptoms and for overall functioning.
2 Psychotherapy can be brief, and there is no evidence that it has to be lengthy to be effective.
3 Psychotherapy works best when it makes use of the common factors in all treatments, while techniques are less important.
4 There are few differences in outcome between specific forms of evidence-based therapy.
5 Some patients, especially those with problematic personality traits, do not respond to standard methods, and need specialized therapies.

Can Psychotherapy Change Personality?

Therapists have grappled with this question since the heyday of psychoanalysis. Freud had little or nothing to say about personality. In their original forms, most psychological therapies have aimed to remove symptoms. That was the focus of behavior therapy (BT) but is also one reason why BT was eventually replaced by cognitive behavioral therapy (CBT).

While CBT also focuses on symptoms, it aims to modify the mental processing of experiences. Beck et al (2001) wrote a book about the treatment of PDs, largely based on methods of changing dysfunctional beliefs.

Classical CBT needs to be modified when applied to personality and PDs. Adaptations of newer methods, focusing on problematic traits, have earned significant research support (Hayes and Hoffman, 2021; Linehan, 2014).

To understand how psychotherapy can be used for modifying traits, we can begin with evidence that personality is not entirely fixed. Literature reviews (Bagby et al, 2016; Harkness and Lilienfeld, 1997) confirm that traits, as measured by the FFM, can change enough to have clinical effects from psychotherapy, particularly through reductions in Neuroticism. As Bagby et al (2016, p. 365) has proposed, traits can also be used as a guide to therapy,

> ... personality assessment can (a) inform where to focus change efforts, (b) foster realistic expectations of therapeutic gains, (c) facilitate effective treatment matching, and (d) enhance self-development ... .We believe positive treatment is optimized if psychotherapists or other providers of intervention are equipped with information from personality assessment to select treatment modalities and construct treatment plans.

Evidence-based therapies are particularly necessary for patients with complex symptoms and pathological trait profiles. The most difficult patients we treat often meet criteria for PDs. For this population, the development of dialectical behavior therapy (DBT, Linehan, 1993) showed that this population is treatable, particularly when therapy focuses on improving emotion regulation. Other key modules in DBT include distress tolerance, mindfulness, and interpersonal effectiveness. Treatment for PDs using DBT skills has been supported by a metanalysis of clinical trials (Cristea et al, 2017). But it is not the only evidence-based option for BPD, and these skills are not unique to DBT. As will be discussed below, a method called a "Unified Protocol" (UP) applies the methods of CBT to modify high levels of neuroticism (Barlow et al, 2014).

These methods, as well as most others that prioritize interventions for managing emotions, fit in with what has been called a "third wave" of cognitive therapy (Hayes and Hofmann, 2021). Its hallmark is a focus on the *person* who experiences symptoms.

DBT has had the largest body of empirical support from clinical trials but has not shown to be more effective than other methods (Storebø et al, 2020). It might even have greater impact if, given its length and need for skilled human resources, the treatment was brief and less expensive. DBT has been studied for a length of 12 months, but its duration can be much shorter (McMain et al, 2022).

Our own programs, applied to BPD, are an adaptation of DBT for brief therapy and are part of a larger program of *stepped care*, that is, offering patients more or less treatment depending on severity (Paris, 2022). We offer a 12-week course of individual and group therapy focusing on emotion regulation and have published effectiveness data in a large sample (Laporte et al, 2018). A similar program, called BPD Compass, offers 18 sessions of individual therapy focusing on reducing neuroticism, has recently been supported by a clinical trial (Sauer-Zavala et al, 2023).

In recent years, DBT has been applied as a "transdiagnostic" intervention for all categories of mental disorder in which emotions are dysregulated, such as addictions, anxiety disorders, and depression (Lungu and Linehan, 2016). And since so many of the patients we see have high neuroticism, teaching skills to manage emotions has become a standard for effective treatment for many disorders with that profile. Essentially, patients need to slow down, contain anxiety, and practice exercises such as mindfulness to calm down and reappraise stressors.

DBT principles have also been adapted for treatment for PD patients with traits of high conscientiousness, with or without neuroticism. This method, called "radically open DBT", is designed for people who suffer from obsessive-compulsive PDs or perfectionistic traits (Lynch et al, 2015).

All these developments involve focusing on trait profiles rather than on symptoms alone (Zilchla-Mano, 2021). We need a better classification of PDs that points to the right choice of treatment. While it is possible that psychotherapy could be more successful if guided by dimensional models of personality, this hypothesis has not been directly tested.

Consider as an example the much-discussed category of narcissistic personality disorder (NPD; Weinberg and Ronningstam, 2022), describing patients who are grandiose, exploitative, and lack a capacity for self-criticism. We do not see that many patients with this diagnosis, and it is not clear whether we know how to modify their traits. It may be easier to manage patients who suffer inwardly (as in BPD) than those who blame others for problems (as in NPD). Another set of problems is associated with of avoidant PD (AVPD; Weinbrecht et al, 2016), a category that lacks an extensive research base. These patients are resistant to change because they avoid exposure to all environments they experience as stressful.

Working with Traits

The FFM model offers some degree of predictability about the outcome of psychotherapy. A meta-analysis of 99 studies found that, on average, therapy works best in patients with higher extraversion, agreeableness, and conscientiousness, and is less effective in patients with high levels of neuroticism (Bucher et al, 2019). Perhaps this data only confirms a long-held wisdom, discussed above, that patients with less severe problems do better in treatment. The obstacle is that many patients we see have problematic trait profiles—either high neuroticism and/or a mixture of low conscientiousness and antagonism—that interfere with the therapeutic alliance. In that light, the FFM might be considered as a "rough guide" to treatment planning.

In spite of these caveats, let us examine how these principles play out in the treatment of patients with unusually high or low scores on FFM domains. The approach suggested here needs to remain general, as research into applying a trait model to therapy is still at an early stage. Yet the success of therapies which are more active (such as DBT) suggests that clinicians need to move past empathic listening and guide patients to use their traits in more constructive ways.

Personality influences many choices in life, and it can maximize their adaptiveness by choosing environments in which they work, and by avoiding environments that work against them. The process of matching life choices with personality traits has been called "nidotherapy" (Tyrer and Tyrer, 2018). The concept here is to make choices in finding a niche that fits best with one's trait profile. Planning therapy can take these variations into account, particularly if the FFM is applied (Bagby et al, 2016). Here, the basic strategy is that traits can be retained but modified to avoid extremes, and that patients need to try out new behaviors to do so. This view of psychotherapy is not just a toolbox or a bag of tricks, but offers tactful advice to patients as to how to make their personality work for them.

FFM Profiles in Life and in Psychotherapy

Extraversion-Introversion

Extraversion has benefits but does not necessarily predict happiness and success in life. This is particularly the case when it is associated with high levels of neuroticism and/or low conscientiousness, that is, impulsivity (Vittersø, 2001). Extraversion is insufficient for success in work and relationships unless it is associated with a good degree of conscientiousness. To put it another way, it is not enough to be gregarious and optimistic if you are not reliable, cannot handle the ups and downs of life, and not good at making commitments work for you and the people around you. In short, being engaging or charming is insufficient for good functioning. Therapy with extraverts can involve guiding patients to a more balanced view of living in a complex, unpredictable, and not always satisfying world.

By and large, highly extraverted people are protected, at least to some extent, by their broad social networks. But these relationships may not be strong enough to allow for emotional sharing. Moreover, this trait domain is associated with excessive risk taking (Oehler and Wedlich, 2018). Extraverts seek high levels of stimulation from the environment, and risky activities of all kinds can fill that bill. Those who score high on extraversion are more likely to seek extra-pair mating, and have more hospitalizations for accidents (Nettle, 2005a). Extraverts need to find nondestructive ways of taking risks and regulate their need for constant social affirmation at the expense of intimacy.

Highly introverted people have an opposite problem. If this trait is only somewhat elevated, lives can be successfully lived by spending more time on solitary pursuits. But when introversion is extreme, risk aversion can lead to painful social isolation (Nettle, 2005). The advantages of introversion are not always obvious, but those who have this trait value having time by themselves. Thus, people who are introverted can avoid unnecessary dependency on others by doing more things alone—such as reading, going to museums, or listening to music. (Those of us who write books also benefit from a niche that rewards introversion.) Therapy with introverted people involves helping them to find a niche in life where they can work productively with fewer social connections.

Neuroticism

Worrying about bad things that might happen can be problematic, but it is not always a bad strategy, as there are many dangers in human life. Not worrying enough can be a factor in wrong decisions accompanied by unjustified over-confidence. (Examples from politics and the history of warfare come to mind here.)

Neuroticism plays a major role in many forms of psychopathology. Once again, this trait domain tends to be a villain in the drama of life. It often stands in the way of functioning and flourishing. But a medium dose of anxiety protects people from unnecessary and unproductive mistakes in work and relationships.

Much of the work clinicians do in therapy centers focuses on curbing the excesses of neuroticism. These traits can be measured by brief version of the Difficulties in Emotion Regulation scale (Victor and Klonsky, 2016). Managing this trait usually involves processing emotions by making them less intense, leading to *distress tolerance*. That is why methods based on the principles and skills of emotion regulation have come to prominence (Kramer, 2000a). These skills mainly involve learning to tolerate negative emotions and/or specific ways of regulation such as mindfulness.

What we see in patients is that emotion dysregulation leads to problems in work and relationships, often ending in a defensive pattern of avoidance that makes life less worth living. To locate emotional regulation in the context of neuroscience, we may be training people to make better use of the prefrontal cortex while not allowing the limbic system to run the show (Messina et al, 2021). And contrary to what many clinicians believe, significant degrees of change in neuroticism can be accomplished in brief therapy (Kramer et al, 2020).

Barlow et al (2014, 2020) have proposed a similar idea, a UP for all disorders characterized by high levels of neurotic traits. These authors recommend that therapy for many patients should focus more on trait neuroticism and less on symptoms. They have published research showing that doing so can be more efficacious for many patents than the symptom-focused approach of classical CBT (Barlow et al, 2021). But we only have a few studies demonstrating the application of the UP to PDs (Fruhbauerova et al, 2024).

The UP is essentially a form of CBT but differs from classical cognitive therapy in its focus on traits. The goal of UP is to process emotions and not be overwhelmed by them. Sauer-Savala and colleagues suggest that this method can be more closely linked to FFM profiles than to diagnostic categories. Based on this theory, her group conducted a clinical trial of 18 individual sessions form BPD called "BPD Compass" (Sauer-Savala et al, 2023) which resembles the brief therapy that our research group has found to be effective for BPD patients.

The UP protocol includes five modules: (1) mindful emotion awareness, (2) cognitive flexibility, (3) identifying and preventing patterns of emotion avoidance, (4) increasing awareness and tolerance of emotion-related physical sensations, and (5) situational emotion-focused exposures. Thus, the UP is similar to DBT, but without the extensive toolbox described by Linehan (2014). Its efficacy for neuroticism, mainly in anxiety and depression, has now been supported by a meta-analysis (Longley and Gleiser, 2023).

Note that this view of neuroticism does not fully account for why this domain underlies so many different clinical pictures, including anxiety disorders, depression, and PDs. Perhaps analysis at a facet level could help. But neurotic symptoms are usually transdiagnostic. That is why anti-depressant medications have such a wide spectrum of efficacy and why they tend to be more potent when prescribed for anxiety than for depression (Bandelow et al, 2015). These agents might better be called "anti-neurotics", and their overlap within a larger domain applies as much to psychotherapy as to pharmacotherapy.

Conscientiousness-Impulsivity

Conscientiousness is usually a good trait to have. It only becomes dysfunctional at an extreme, when perfectionism dominates behavior, leading to paralysis and indecisiveness. There are situations in life where snap decisions need to be made. A favorite example among evolutionary psychologists is a scenario where a hunter-gatherer hears a noise in the grass and has to quickly decide whether to flee from a predator or dismiss the sound as unthreatening. Modern life rewards conscientiousness, which pays off when working in an office, and can be as useful as it was for hunters during the Pleistocene era.

As we have seen, being conscientious is important for success in life. People take note of who is (and who isn't) reliable and judge them accordingly. Being low on this domain means that one's lifestyle can be unpredictable, chaotic, and impulsive.

Treating impulsivity is one of the more difficult tasks for psychotherapists. It involves teaching patients how to recognize emotions, but to be cautious about acting on them. The sense of urgency that is associated with impulsivity needs to be curbed and controlled. Doing so requires a good deal of practice. Methods for managing impulsivity need to be among the procedures in a therapist's toolbox. But you have to convince patients to stop doing things that work rapidly but only temporarily (Miller and Rollnick, 2012). They can then find better ways of regulating themselves. But as most therapists know, that is easier said than done! This is one of the reasons why DBT skills have become widely applied in many types of therapy for patients who have difficulties with traits (Eeles and Walker, 2022).

Agreeableness and Antagonism

Being agreeable is almost always better than being antagonistic. But too high a level of this trait can be associated with problems maintaining boundaries in work and relationships. If not managed properly, interpersonal failures occur and can eventually end in social isolation.

Therapy itself is not feasible without a good degree of agreeableness on both sides. Patients have to show up, tell their stories, and be open to feedback on what they are doing wrong and could do differently. And therapists have to play their part by being tactful and nonjudgmental. These are among the basic ingredients for a therapeutic alliance.

In a social world, while most people are trustworthy, there are always predators out to take advantage of you. For this reason. protecting yourself requires being appropriately disagreeable or antagonistic at certain times. I have worked with patients who were so desperate for love that they ignored obvious red flags and were often attracted to toxic partners who were successful predators who knew how to push other people's buttons. Therapy with overly agreeable people needs to teach them how to identify overly dominant friends and partners before they become toxic. But therapy with antagonistic people is even more challenging. That is because these patients can be disagreeable in treatment and drop out of therapy.

Openness

Openness is relatively neutral to the risk for psychopathology and is rarely the focus of psychological treatment. But this trait can still cause trouble at its extremes. To be overly open to experience can be a problem if your emotional needs lead you to make bad or dangerous choices. Too much openness, particularly when linked with neuroticism, runs the risk of being guided by misinformation, such as conspiracy theories. But to be overly closed can be linked with being imperceptive, unobservant, and short-sighted (Woo et al, 2014).

Modifying Traits in Clinical Practice

Modifying Neuroticism

There are now several well-documented ways to lower problem-atic levels of neuroticism (Linehan, 2014; Sauer-Zavala et al, 2017). Essentially, patients first need to understand the role of emotions in their lives, and to recognize them before they get out of hand. They can then apply specific skills (e.g., mindfulness) to calm themselves down. Patients need to not only stop avoiding situations that trigger a strong emotional response, but also to learn how to tolerate negative responses and to regulate them.

Modifying Extraversion-Introversion

Research on extraversion has mainly focused on problems associated with risk taking, which can affect behavior in the workplace, in intimate relationships, and in a family (Nettle, 2005b). If conscientiousness is low, impulsive behavior patterns can begin to appear. This picture requires a therapy with a strong element of psychoeducation.

Introversion can be adaptive but when excessive, as in avoidant PD, becomes a problem (Granneman, 2017). We are a social species, and intro-verts are at risk for loneliness. Again, while it can be more difficult for patients to develop new behaviors than to give up old ones, therapy can aim to encourage a gradual widening of social networks.

Modifying Conscientiousness-Impulsivity

For high conscientiousness, patients need to reduce their need for control. The method of radically open behavior therapy teaches patients to be open to new experiences and points of view, making control more flexible, and encouraging openness to intimacy (Lynch, 2018).

Again, managing impulsivity is one of the more difficult tasks in therapy. In DBT (Linehan, 1993), it is mainly a way of trying to deal with negative emotions (as in self-harm, suicidality, substance use). Emotion regulation can also be the key to controlling impulsive actions.

Modifying Agreeableness-Antagonism

As discussed above, some people are too agreeable, in which case therapy needs to teach them to build up better boundaries, and to watch out for red flags that warn of exploitation. These patients try to buy love but may not feel lovable. They need to find a middle ground.

In contrast, antagonism is a more difficult problem, and not much is known about its management (Lynam and Miller, 2019). These patients may only get better if they can find a way trust their therapist. That could allow them to try new patterns of behavior that open the door to better interpersonal relationships.

Personality as a Predictor of Failure in Psychotherapy

Psychotherapy provides effective treatment for most common mental disorders, with outcomes that compare well to medication in depression or anxiety. But not all patients do well in therapy. The presence of treatment failures has led some clinicians to think that if symptoms have been present for many years, therapy also needs to be long. But there is little or no evidence supporting extended courses of psychotherapies.

There is a limited amount of research to determine whether the FFM can be used to predict the outcome of psychological treatment, as suggested by Bagby et al (2016). However, we have come to realize that personality trait profiles account for many treatment failures (Bucher et al, 2019).

One reason is that most of the patients we see are high in neuroticism.

Widiger and Oltmanns (2017) described the prevalence of this trait as a public health problem. I prefer to see it as part of the human condition. This trait creates even more problems when neuroticism interacts with other domains. As we saw in Chapter 8, the combination of this domain with impulsivity and antagonism is what the FFM would identify as a PD.

If every patient had these difficulties, work as a psychotherapist would be even more challenging than it already is. Fortunately, that is not the case. We know that most patients, whatever their traits or mental disorders can benefit from therapy (Markham et al, 2019; Wampold, 2015). But more specific methods are often needed to modify the problematic traits of PDs to make them manageable.

Let us now consider some examples, highlighting the relationship between FFM profiles and *DSM* diagnoses of PDs.

Clinical Examples

The reader will note that the outcomes in these cases are variable. Unlike other books on therapy, I aimed to avoid describing only clear successes. This practice may encourage clinicians to treat difficult patients, and can be discouraging to clinicians who are not easily satisfied with partial remissions. But miracles are exceptional in therapy. Instead, I have aimed to illustrate the realities of clinical practice. The majority of treatments lead to partial but meaningful outcomes, but once PD patients are on the road to recovery, they usually go on to improve further (Zanarini, 2019). I have, therefore, chosen six examples, of which four can be counted as clearly positive, two-thirds being same percentage who recovered in our effectiveness trial.

Example 1: Neuroticism and Introversion

Georgina was a woman in her middle 20s, referred to our clinic after a failed treatment for binge eating disorder. She also had a long history of self-harm, cutting herself since early adolescence. She described her family as having provided stability but showed little interest in her emotions. Georgina often experienced suicidal ideation, for which she had been seen on several occasions in the ER.

In the past, Georgina had been involved with toxic partners who abused her verbally and physically. She had few friends, but was functioning in a long-term stable relationship with a man who did not mind looking after her. Georgina had worked as a nurse in several community clinics, but kept moving from one job to another, and had long had problems finding a satisfying direction in life.

Therapy helped Georgina to observe her mood swings, and she benefited from the use of mindfulness exercises taught in group therapy. (Georgina had long been interested in Buddhism.) Georgina also benefited from individual therapy, and was able to use what she learned to move into a different job where she found colleagues with whom she could connect. She was no longer considering suicide or self-harm.

DSM-5-TR Diagnosis: BPD

Example 2: Neuroticism and Impulsivity

Melanie was a university student who was highly sensitive to her environment. She had grown up in a climate of emotional neglect, with parents who were well-meaning but unresponsive. Melanie had been oppositional as a child, both in school and at home. Things got worse after puberty, when she began to use drugs, and to have unstable relationships as well as sex with inappropriate partners. As an adult, this pattern continued, falling "in love" with men she hardly knew, and then being repeatedly abandoned by them. Melanie feared abandonment lacked the capacity to be patient and get to know partners before making an emotional commitment. When these relationships fell apart, she made several suicide attempts by overdose.

Melanie learned how to identify emotions in therapy, and how to tolerate emotions without acting on them. This skill allowed her to stay in school, where she eventually trained as a social worker. Given the validation she gained from her job, she became less dependent on male attention and sexual attraction. Melanie gained skills at picking up red flags early, and on discharge was in a relationship with a man who was more reliable.

DSM-5-TR Diagnosis: BPD

Example 3: Neuroticism and Introversion

Ann had suffered from chronic worry ever since childhood, and her problems continued into adulthood. She never found close friends and felt inadequate in every social situation. Ann had lived with a man for several years, but due to her anxiety, they almost never had sexual relations. She had a part-time job in a woman's shelter, but had gone on a long leave of absence leading to further social isolation. Due to panic attacks, Ann became somewhat agoraphobic. She sought therapy and was seen for a year in our clinic. Ann managed to return to her job, but only on a part time basis. Ann never took the risks required to change her traits and remained locked in an avoidant pattern.

DSM-5-TR Diagnosis: Avoidant PD

Example 4: Neuroticism and Conscientiousness

Paula was trained as a nurse but was unable to practice her profession. This was mainly due to her perfectionism, which did not allow her to make rapid decisions for patients under her care. She feared errors and would repeatedly check to be sure she had not given the wrong medications. Her anxiety made her disorganized and slow. As a result, Paula took an administrative desk job, where bad decisions could never be fatal. She lived in her own apartment and had a limited social life. In therapy, Paula seemed more interested in control than in change, coming into every session with reprints of articles on the web that would justify her own sense of what was wrong. Paula had arranged neuropsychological testing for attention-deficit hyperactivity disorder, but the results were equivocal. Actually, she had done consistently well in school—until she had to practice what she learned in a classroom.

Therapy helped Paula to be less of a perfectionist, and she kept her desk job. She was advised to expand her circle of friends, which she did, providing her with more emotional support.

DSM-5-TR Diagnosis: Obsessive-Compulsive PD

Example 5: Extraversion and Agreeableness

Barbara was a charming young woman with many friends. She was rarely alone and felt most comfortable in a large group. When Barbara went to university, she studied best in noisy coffee shops. She also was something of a thrill seeker and enjoyed bungee jumping.

Barbara spent several years in a relationship with a charismatic drug dealer who emotionally abused her. She tried to please him, and she always went back even when he was flagrantly unfaithful. She never considered suicide. In retrospect, Barbara felt she had usually put on an act for other people, and rarely expressed her true feelings. In therapy, she was advised to avoid intimate relationships for a few months until she felt in better control of her emotions and behaviors. Barbara was encouraged to spend more time building relationships with other women, which provided validation in a more manageable context and to concentrate on her studies.

DSM-5-TR Diagnosis: Unspecified PD

Example 6: Antagonism and Conscientiousness

Caitlin was a valued employee in a business corporation. When there was a problem, everyone looked to her to sort things out. But she had very few friends, and her relationships with men always ended in disappointment. For several years, loneliness had made Caitlin obsessed with the thought of suicide and had even considered writing a will. She had little connection with family, from whom she was almost entirely estranged. Caitlin was the only child of an alcoholic mother and an absent father. She had studied violin, and her only pleasure in life was attending classical music concerts. She asked for therapy hoping to find a reason for living. However, Caitlin spent most of the sessions explaining to her therapist why what he had to say was wrong, and did not benefit from treatment.

DSM-5-TR Diagnosis: Unspecified PD

I worked in specialized clinics for PDs for 25 years and learned to be satisfied with partial but meaningful results. We discharged patients who had the tools to continue improved functioning while being their own therapist. We were satisfied if our patient learned to use therapy to find a place in the world, and to build meaningful close relationships. But not all the people we see benefit, as we know from the psychotherapy research literature (Lampropoulos, 2011). Moreover, attempts to change personality profiles in radical ways by seeing patients for years instead of months is not an evidence-based procedure.

Finding a Niche

Psychotherapy is a kind of education. The "course curriculum" consists of showing patients how to make better and more adaptive use of their personality traits. One of the main principles of pedagogy in various domains is that learning is more effective if it takes place in a real-life setting. When treating people with personality pathology, the "seminar" of psychotherapy takes place in the therapist's office, but the "laboratory" takes place outside these sessions. Encouraging patients to learn new behaviors is the "homework".

Although psychotherapists often eschew offering *explicit* educational interventions, much of what they do involves an *implicit* education. Simply by deciding what to focus on in therapy, we send our patients a message. Most therapists routinely encourage patients to try new ways of coping with problems. But personality-disordered patients, locked into repetitive maladaptive behaviors, need an active therapeutic technique. We need not be afraid of teaching the skills that patients lack.

There are several ways to teach patients how to work with traits. One can generally begin with *modifying maladaptive behaviors*. Patients are asked from the beginning to identify something destructive (e.g., cutting, substance abuse) and to focus on stopping it during treatment. In this way, therapists help patients to recognize maladaptive traits, as well as the negative emotions they experience. They then need to apply their personality traits more judiciously and selectively to environmental challenges. For example, most therapies aim to curb excessive levels of neuroticism, and teach patients to identify emotions and to regulate them. In patients who suffer consequences for impulsivity, therapists must work to reduce the intensity and frequency of these behaviors.

Some personality traits are easier to modify than others. Thus, it may be much easier to help a compulsive patient to work less, than to get an impulsive patient to find a niche in life or getting a stable job. It may also be easier to help patients who have conflicts in relationships to handle them better than to get those who have few or no relationships to avoid the risk of rejection. More generally, patients must face situations that make them anxious and give up avoidant strategies that do not work.

Another way by which therapists can work with traits is to learn how to make better use of them by capitalizing on the strong points of their personality. This usually involves the principle of "nidotherapy" (Tyrer and Tyrer, 2018)—selecting environments in which their traits will be useful.

For example, individuals with high levels of neuroticism, extraversion, and impulsivity, or any combination of these traits, can benefit from choosing an environment in which rapid responses are useful. Some possible career choices could include entering the military, joining the police, becoming a fire fighter, working in a hospital emergency room, or becoming a stockbroker. Even if an occupation is irremediably predictable, an impulsive person might take up sublimations, such as sky diving. At the same time, people with these traits should avoid environments in which rapid responses are a palpable handicap. For example, highly impulsive individuals may not be well suited to working in a bureaucracy.

In contrast, individuals with high levels of neuroticism with social anxiety can benefit from maximizing predictability in their life. They might, therefore, want to choose occupations that reward careful, slow, and persistent effort, and that reward working alone. Examples could include being a librarian, a software engineer, or an accountant. If they also have a stable social network, they will suffer less from social avoidance. When anxiety falls to manageable levels, people with introversion can be productive. To return to an example of personal significance, people who write books need less stimulation from others and feel comfortable working alone for long periods, supported by an intimate relationship with a word processor.

Highly emotional individuals can benefit from working in settings where emotional reactivity is more useful. This could mean choosing occupations that involve working directly with people, and where a combination of emotionality and openness to experience can be associated with empathy, as well as the effective communication skills of a "people person". Although working with other people usually requires putting empathy under conscious control, people who are themselves unemotional tend not to be effective in working with the feelings of others.

There has been some interest among clinicians in the concept of "personalized psychotherapy" (Zilcha-Mano, 2021). In medicine, personalized treatment usually refers to the genome, to biological markers, or to a response to specific medications. But in clinical psychology, this construct can be applied to personality traits. Even when a patient is locked into maladaptive behavior patterns, therapists can recommend an alternative set of behaviors consistent with their personality profile.

These conclusions show why personality assessment provides a useful overall framework for identifying key problems and planning therapy. Yet working with people to modify traits is required to attain success in work and relationships is a complex business, and outcomes are not always predictable. The most general principle is that when traits are sufficiently intense to produce dysfunction, moving them from one end of a spectrum to a safer middle ground is in order. Again, the clinically most important targets are high levels of neuroticism and impulsivity.

The reader will note that the model recommended here is closer to CBT than to a psychodynamic model. Yet therapy remains a place for exploring life histories, which always need to be validated. You just need to avoid the mistake of attributing every outcome to "trauma". That popular idea among therapists ignores entirely the role of biology in psychopathology. The concept of personality, based on gene–environment interactions, should be an antidote to the trauma fad (Paris, 2023a).

Making use of histories in this way can also be linked to the crucial DBT concept of *radical acceptance* (Linehan, 1993), in which the past is fully acknowledged, but patients are encouraged to move on to develop a vision of a different future. In an integrative psychotherapy, the message to patients is something like this: "Yes, you have often been mistreated and misunderstood in the past, but that need not prevent you from having a better life now and in the future".

Chapter 10

Access to Treatment for Personality Disorders

Psychotherapy in Health Care Systems

As the last chapter recommended, evidence-based treatment of PDs requires specialized forms of psychotherapy designed to modify trait profiles. However, this form of treatment, in spite of its effectiveness and efficacy, is often unavailable in health care systems (Paris, 2020).

Many countries have governmental insurance that aim to ensure that all citizens have access to mental health care. However, this mandate does not necessarily cover psychotherapy. The UK, Continental Europe, and Australia offer some coverage, but it remains spotty. For example, the UK National Health Service insures cognitive behavioral therapy for anxiety and depression (Clarke, 2018), but not for PDs. In the USA, insurance tends to be private, and specialized psychotherapies that last for more than a few sessions are rarely covered. In Canada, where the governmental insurance system is committed in principle to universal coverage, psychiatrists rarely have openings for new patients (Gratzer and Goldbloom, 2016), while psychologists are not covered at all.

The problem is not limited to psychotherapy. Mental health services of all kinds are rarely adequately funded or staffed. The most likely explanation is the continued stigma that accompanies mental disorders of all kinds. This view is often accompanied by doubts about the efficacy of psychotherapy. And patients who have mental disorders are not good at advocacy.

Health care systems also do not always follow specific guidelines, based on research findings, as to whether treatments are evidence-based, or as to which treatments are most effective. Instead, they reflect standard practices approved by experts. The aspects of treatment most likely to be insured consist largely of initial evaluations and medication prescriptions, followed by checkups.

Since psychiatry entered the era of evidence-based practice, clinical trials now support a range of psychotherapies that are both specific to disorders

DOI: 10.4324/9781003519942-10

and that are time-limited. They show that talking therapy can be just as efficacious as medication. But most psychotherapists are not psychiatrists. We need to provide insurance to cover the work of allied mental health professionals. Ideally, doing so should be done in an institutional setting where the effects of therapy can be measured and monitored.

Given that empirical evidence supports brief therapy (20 sessions or less), this need not be an expensive investment. Moreover, if evidence-based therapies get people back to work faster, insurance systems would almost certainly save money. In other words, psychotherapy is *cost-effective* (Lazar, 2014).

The exclusion of psychotherapies from coverage by public insurance, and its limited coverage by private insurance, continues in many countries in spite of strong evidence for their efficacy, effectiveness, and cost-effectiveness. Government officials and private insurers seem to be largely unaware of research findings on psychological treatment. Instead, they seem to share the widely held view that psychotherapies are lengthy and ineffective. They perceive talking therapy as a bottomless pit of costs and see drug prescriptions as less of a drain on the system. But evidence-based psychotherapy should be an essential part of any comprehensive treatment plan that should be readily accessible to people with mental disorders (Clarke, 2018).

In high-prevalence common mental disorders, such as anxiety and mild-to-moderate major depression, psychotherapy and medication yield much the same outcome (DeRubeis et al, 2008). But in more complex illnesses, particularly eating disorders (Bhadoria et al, 2010), substance use disorders (Walters and Rotgers, 2012), and PDs (Paris, 2020a), medication has a more limited role, and specialized psychotherapies are the most effective interventions. This raises the stakes to provide access to psychological treatment.

The perception that psychotherapy is resource-intensive and ruinously expensive is incorrect. Most therapy in practice is time-limited and focused on current problems. For this reason, treatments with a strong evidence base can be insured without breaking the bank. The much more expensive alternative of long-term open-ended therapy (lasting for more than a year) has not never been subjected to rigorous clinical trials. For that reason, this kind of treatment should not be routinely insured.

Slowly but surely, recognition of research findings has led to increased support for psychotherapy. A good first step has been made in the UK under the National Health Service, which makes uses of trained psychotherapists (Clarke, 2018), This program, called Improving Access to Psychological Therapies (IAPT), has been available for well over a decade. All patients are monitored and followed to determine the outcome of treatment, with encouraging results. IAPT is designed to make CBT available for anxiety or mood disorders—but not for PDs.

However, patients with more complex psychopathology require more specialized therapies. This is particularly the case for eating disorders, substance use disorders, and PDs. A survey of services for PDs in England found that while most clinics have some dedicated services for PD patients, there is great variability in availability, and quality of care remains uncertain. Evidence-based therapies for complex disorders in the UK are mainly accessible in the private sector.

However, there is encouraging news from a position paper by the Royal College of Psychiatrists (2020) that advocates better training for professionals involved in the management of PD patients at all levels of care. Hopefully, this recommendation will be taken up by the NHS, and its fate will be different from earlier proposals (that were mainly applied to forensic cases).

The Length of Psychotherapy for PDs

PDs are a major public health problem. Most surveys find that they affect about 10% of the general population (Paris, 2010). The category that creates the greatest demand for treatment is BPD, which has a community prevalence of about 1–2% (Trull et al, 2010) and a clinical prevalence that can reach 9% (Zimmerman et al, 2005).

We have known for several decades years that BPD is treatable with evidence-based psychotherapies, and these findings have been confirmed by meta-analyses (Cristea et al, 2017; Oud et al, 2018) as well as by systematic reviews from the Cochrane Collaboration (Binks et al, 2006). Given the burden of this illness, one would think that access to therapy for these patients would be a priority for the mental health system. Yet that is not the case. By and large, the current treatments for BPD, while much more effective than what was available in the past, are difficult to access for patients who are not wealthy.

The role of psychotherapy in the treatment of PDs has changed greatly in recent decades. There was a time when open-ended therapy was widely recommended for complex problems, on the assumption that long-term disorders require long-term treatment. But research has not found that approach to be efficacious (Paris, 2020a). Clinicians can now choose from a number of evidence-based and time-limited options: cognitive behavioral therapy (CBT, Davidson et al, 2006), dialectical behavior therapy (DBT; Linehan, 1993), mentalization-based therapy (MBT; Bateman and Fonagy, 2004), schema-focused therapy (SFT; Giesen-Bloo et al, 2006), transference-focused psychotherapy (TFP; Yeomans et al, 2002), and systems training for emotional predictability and problem solving (STEPPS, Blum et al, 2008). For the problems associated with BPD, DBT has been backed up by the most research (Paris, 2025).

But many of these options are too lengthy to be accessible. The original form of DBT, involving at least a year of group and individual therapy, and often much longer, can be as expensive as psychoanalysis. Even if this kind of therapy were available in the public sector, its length and need for human resources would quickly fills up slots and create waiting lists.

The situation would be different if insurers knew that therapy does not need to be lengthy therapy is understandable. In North America, employee health plans may pay for only 6 sessions. But that number of sessions falls below the minimum (12–20) that has long been supported by efficacy and effectiveness research (Lambert, 2007; Mackenzie, 1996). Moreover, therapy for PDs is cost-effective (Meuldijk et al, 2018). When patients improve, they can return to work and will not require expensive emergency room visits or hospital admissions.

More recent forms of treatment for BPD avoid being open-ended. Research suggests that, with a clear structure and well-defined goals, it can be effective within just a few months (Laporte et al, 2018). Some PD patients may not respond to brief therapy, but it should be tried first on most patients who come to clinical attention. In a stepped care program, longer therapy can be offered to this population, but should not last more than 12 months (Paris, 2017).

For medical treatment, while economic constraints can trump public health concerns, governments and private insurance will support the funding many expensive options. Consider the high cost of renal dialysis or cancer chemotherapy. These conditions do not have the same stigma as mental illness in general (Corrigan and Watson, 2002), or PDs in particular. Finally, funding policies reflect our admiration for high-tech medicine. Psychotherapies are low-tech, making it easier to perceive them as unscientific.

The current situation is that any program that offers therapy lasting for more than a year quickly becomes closed to new patients. The result is waiting lists. This practice does not meet the needs of patients who enter the mental health system—and PD patients are not good at waiting.

In summary, if we want to open up access to treatment, brief and less resource-intensive programs are our best bet. Shorter therapies should be the "default" condition, with longer therapies held in reserve for particularly difficult cases. A classic study of psychotherapy in a large clinical sample with various diagnoses found that the majority of patients had a rapid decline in symptoms within the first few weeks. (Patients even improved prior to the first session, in anticipation of help.) The researchers observed an asymptotic flattening of the response curve around the 20-week mark, after which patients improved very slowly. But the sub-group in this cohort who had problematic personality traits did not benefit from longer treatment. While this study was conducted decades ago, no further research has changed its conclusions. A more recent study of patients with BPD found no difference when patients were assigned to either 6 months or 12 months of therapy.

The idea that complex psychopathology must require extended courses of therapy is not evidence-based. But some metanalyses aim to bolster the claim that complex disorders (such as PDs) need long-term therapy (Leichsenring and Rabung, 2008, 2011). But given a limited data base, small samples, and small effect sizes in these studies, one cannot reach any broad conclusions. In theory, it would be possible to carry out better studies, using larger samples, and/or random assignment to therapies of varying duration. But the cost of this research would be high, and given the current climate of psychiatric research (in which priority is generally given to neuroscience), it is unlikely that a study of this kind would be funded.

How Psychotherapy Became Lengthy

How did psychotherapy become lengthy? That was not the original aim of either Sigmund Freud or Aaron Beck. Psychoanalysis became "interminable" when therapists adopted the idea that when therapy has not helped, one just has to go on longer. The result is what Freud (1937) himself called "interminable" treatment. CBT also began as a time-limited therapy, and the clinical trials that have supported it were carried out over a few months. However, since therapists in practice are not subject to constraints, it is not unusual for CBT patients to be treated for years.

Some patients *like* going to therapists, and if they can pay for it, there is a market for that kind of service. (This scenario may seem a bit extreme, but I have seen quite a few patients who remained in therapy for life.) If you have money, weekly psychotherapy can be as much of a routine as a trip to the hairdresser. Moreover, the longer patients stay, the better are the financial prospects for privately funded therapists whose relatively high fees can make filling slots in their schedule problematic.

The use of long-term therapy for PDs was rooted in the idea that patients have problems that can only be worked on over time. But extended courses of treatment can also be harmful, at least for some patients (Barlow, 2010). Excessive dependence on therapy has a way of encouraging stasis and regression. Patients who continue treatment indefinitely can end up as "lifers" who never terminate therapy (Horwitz, 1974).

CBT (Beck et al, 2015) was designed as a brief treatment, and the clinical trials that support it lasted for a few months. But all therapies have a tendency to drift, particularly in circumstances where acute symptoms have resolved, and when patients or therapists are not satisfied. If patients have insurance or can afford therapy, treatment runs the danger of lasting for years.

Careful reviews of the psychotherapy literature over several decades show no empirical support for therapies that last for much more than six months (Lambert, 2007; Mackenzie, 1996). We need to conduct more trials comparing psychotherapy for BPD in brief vs. extended forms. In a recent example, when dialectical behavior therapy was provided randomly to patients in 6-month or 12-month packages, there was no difference in outcome, either at the end of therapy or at two-year follow-up (McMain et al, 2022).

As it stands, the length of treatment tends to be determined by the theoretical views of those who originate the method. Even in therapies like DBT that have a good evidence base, more ambitious goals for change, requiring years of therapy, have never been supported by research.

The burden of proof lies not with those who favor brief intervention, but with those who favor lengthy and costly treatments. Although extended courses of psychotherapy for mental disorders have become less common in practice (Mojtabai and Olfson, 2008), brief adaptations of long-term interventions have been applied to several types of psychological treatment. One example is short-term dynamic psychotherapy, whose efficacy has been supported by clinical trials on a wide range of patients, with results comparable to CBT (Leichsenring et al, 2004). These successes may not, however, be due to "interpretations" favored by those who practice this kind of treatment, but to common factors present in all therapies.

Some PD patients retain functional disabilities after the remission of acute symptoms (Zanarini, 2019). But more extended courses of the same treatment have not been shown to resolve these problems. A consistently effective rehabilitation program for chronic patients has yet to be developed and tested.

In summary, evidence-based treatments for PDs, in spite of encouraging results in clinical trials, are not widely accessible. That is not surprising when one considers the prevalence of this disorder. But the problem could be reduced if patients were managed with briefer interventions, reserving longer treatments for those who fail to respond to a first course of therapy.

Two leaders in research on PDs have supported this principle. Zanarini (2009, p. 376) recommends that: "less intensive and less costly forms of treatment need to be developed". Similarly, McMain et al (2009, p. 649) suggest: "given the lack of availability of effective treatments for BPD, research is needed on the effectiveness of less-intensive models of care in order to help inform decisions about the allocation of scarce health care resources".

It does not follow that *any* brief therapy will be effective. The specific principles developed in longer treatments can be adapted for brief treatment. The current state of evidence is weak for long-term therapies, so choosing this option depends on either failure of brief therapy, or on severity and chronicity. If one renounces unrealistic aims such as changing personality traits, less ambitious goals can be set, sensibly limited to the improvement of psychosocial functioning. The goals of therapy need to be modest, aiming to lead patients to a better quality of life.

The way psychotherapy is practiced has been marked by resistance to these principles. Therapists can be comfortable with and attached to the patients they already have. If they practice on a fee-for-service basis, they may not be sure they can fill their schedules if they discharge patients.

Practices focusing on long-term therapy can be comfortable for psychiatrists and psychologists who work on their own in an office outside an institution. Some clinicians run a practice where patients are seen weekly for years, with new clients only occasionally taken. But if open-ended treatment is not evidence-based, it should not be a default option for practitioners.

Costing Psychotherapy

We live in an age where almost anything that requires human resources can be viewed as expensive. (That is why professionals have learned to do without secretaries.) The rule seems to be that if time is money, then services that require human resources will be too costly. It takes a few minutes to write a prescription. Evidence-based psychotherapy requires regular sessions that are long enough for a thorough discussion of problems. If that kind of treatment goes on for a year or more, it will indeed be expensive.

While the evidence that psychotherapy is efficacious is extensive, it is less well-known that psychological treatment is also highly cost-effective (Lazar, 2014). As discussed earlier, there are several reasons for cost-saving. First, patients who get better and stay better require less care after remission. Second, research shows that patients in therapy are less likely to seek expensive medical investigations, and less likely to go to emergency rooms. Third, patients who benefit from psychotherapy usually go back to work more rapidly. For all these reasons, investing in psychotherapy provides benefits beyond the treatment itself.

Cost-effectiveness has been researched and can be quantified. Several studies have shown that access to psychotherapy for patients with PDs leads to a cost saving (Meuldijk et al, 2018; Soeteman et al, 2010; Wetzelaer et al, 2016). A systematic review (O'Sullivan et al, 2017) has confirmed these findings. Brief therapies are the best bet to achieve savings.

But consider the cost for a year of DBT. Patients are seen twice a week, are allowed to page the therapist, and the treatment team meets weekly to review the case. Let us consider the cost for these services, which are at least $200 a week in the USA, and even more in the UK. If a full course of DBT can last several years, the cost without insurance would be at least $10,000 a year. Yet many of our patients have limited education and low-level jobs.

The main reason why there is a market for DBT is that there are wealthy families to pay for it. Yet evidence-based therapies for PDs only describe results after a full year of treatment.

A clinic for PD patients needs therapists with a range of professional backgrounds. All the personnel in our program have a government-approved certificate in psychotherapy. Where I work (in Canada), the health care system offers little or no coverage for psychologists outside hospitals. The only reason that our team has been able to provide out-patient therapy is that psychiatrists, salaried psychologists, and other mental health professionals, as well as a number of students, have given time to providing these services.

When Less Is More

To address the gap between efficacy and availability, we need to separate patients most likely to benefit from those who are less likely to respond. That means applying more resources to acute cases, where therapy is most likely to make a difference. And by keeping treatment brief, we make room for new cases.

Clinicians have a responsibility to help as many people as possible, and to keep waiting lists short. The longer the treatment the less room there will be for new patients. PD patients may get a higher priority when highly trained professionals stop offering psychotherapy to the "worried well", that is, those with minimal levels of dysfunction. That population does not need to be managed by specialized clinicians. And when resources are scarce—as they always are—programs that reduce waiting lists are the best investment.

How many therapists do you need to see patients who comprise 1% of the population for once a week over a year? The answer is many more than are available or are likely to be available. The result is that most patients receive only medication, followed by brief checkups from psychiatrists or family doctors. It is, therefore, not surprising that emergency settings end up seeing a large number of patients with PDs.

The principle of *triage*, originally established in military medicine, suggests that when more patients are sick than can be treated, one divides them into those who will recover with or without treatment, those who will not recover with or without treatment, and those for whom immediate care will make a difference.

Steps to Shortening Psychotherapy

The first step in shortening psychotherapy is a change in philosophy. Therapists have to accept (or, in Linehan's term, to "radically accept") the limitations of what they can do for patients. There is no such thing as a therapeutic utopia. But therapy can help get a life back on track.

A practical goal for the therapy of PD is to get patients on a trajectory of gradual recovery. The McLean Study of Adult Development (MSAD) that followed BPD patients for 24 years describes this pattern, with relapses becoming rare once the recovery process is under way (Zanarini, 2019).

We need to adapt existing methods for use outside specialized clinics. In a dismantling study, Linehan and colleagues found that DBT skills training were a crucial component of the package, raising the possibility that it could be offered separately, without undertaking more expensive courses of treatment. There is even some evidence that brief psychoeducation, based on DBT principles, can reduce symptoms in BPD. A few such programs have also been developed in the UK for PDs (e.g., Huband et al, 2007). There is also some evidence for the efficacy of standard cognitive therapy for PD running for only about 20 sessions (Davidson et al, 2006).

The developers of mentalization-based treatment (MBT) have suggested that a full course of their program may not be necessary. They proposed that the model could be offered more briefly for frontline professionals who do not work in hard-to-access specialized clinics. Similarly, a program called Systems Training for Emotional Predictability and Problem Solving (STEPPS; Blum et al, 2008) was developed to serve patients with little access to specialized care, and has gained research support. This treatment is entirely in groups, and lasts for 20 sessions. It is designed to be an adjunct to treatment as usual, particularly in rural communities where access is typically poor. A course of STEPPS can also be followed by further psychoeducation. While not as widely used as DBT, STEPPS offers a practical and inexpensive alternative.

Another key finding for mental health planning is that hospitalization for BPD patients may either not need to be used or can be kept short.

Effective out-patient therapy produces a cost-saving, and this principle has been shown to apply to the treatment of BPD. Costs might be further reduced by a wider realization among clinicians that hospitalization for BPD is in most cases unnecessary. One of the main reasons why BPD patients are unnecessarily hospitalized is the difficulty of rapid access to evidence-based out-patient services. Moreover, the treatment of BPD can reduce costs to insurers due to absence from work.

In order to carry out any of these programs, we need better insurance. Access is particularly problematic in the USA, given its fragmented health system and limited insurance. Moreover, the current culture of mental health services prefers medication over psychotherapy. This may be less true of Northern European countries. In Germany, specialized psychotherapy programs such as DBT are generously covered by insurance. In the UK, there have been plans to extend the IPAT program to patients with more severe disorders. But specialized treatments may not be conducted in practice settings outside of hospitals. Few mental health professionals have the training required to offer evidence-based therapies.

Yet due to the interest created by DBT, many therapists now know that BPD is treatable and are more likely to make this diagnosis. Recognition might further increase if treatment were more accessible. In general, the care of severely ill patients is not ideal for solo practice but can go better with a multidisciplinary team. Yet even in solo practice, it may be possible to offer effective treatment to most of these cases by shortening therapy and restricting more expensive programs to those who fail to respond to briefer intervention. This is the basis of stepped care programs.

Stepped Care for PDs

A stepped-care model can be of value in conditions such as PDs, in which symptoms remit at variable rates. Since the public health burden of PDs is high, scarce mental health resources need to be triaged. In this way, patients with a PD can "step" into their care, moving in and out of the system, so that only a minority requires continuous long-term treatment (Paris, 2017, 2022).

Stepped care can be seen as a kind of clinical experiment, in which patients are offered different grades of intervention depending on treatment response. Younger patients with acute symptoms, who are more likely to show early recovery, may be the best candidates for brief intervention. That group actually forms the majority of patients seen in clinical settings.

It is well known in psychotherapy research that further gains often take place once formal therapy ends. As with any other set of skills, what is learned with the help of a teacher can also be practiced without one. For this reason, one does not have to wait for full remission before discharging patients to the community (while allowing for re-entry if needed). This sequence, which coordinates primary, secondary, and tertiary care, has been recommended by the Australian guidelines for the treatment of BPD. An American group has made similar recommendations, but have not been formally adopted.

If the first step should fail, patients who fail to improve or who relapse after a short course of therapy can be referred to more intensive time-limited treatment, as in day hospital settings, or to a longer course of treatment in an out-patient clinic. At each step, monitoring of progress works to prevent "drift", and further interventions can be geared to the intermittent course of the disorder. For most patients, such a program will involve one or more acute interventions, as well as availability between episodes.

The most severe and chronic patients, those who use up the most resources and put the most stress on the mental health system, may not always be suitable for brief therapy, but can benefit from referral to a longer program. But this option should also come with a time limit.

The question is how best to make the best use of limited human resources. Stepped care could make services more available and less costly, avoiding continuous follow-up. Providing brief treatment, with only a short waiting list, is usually suitable for patients who present with more acute symptoms and allows specialized PD clinics to be accessible to patients. In our program, the wait for short-term treatment is never more than three months and is usually shorter. A minority of more severe cases, about 20% of the total, may require longer periods of rehabilitation.

But some patients are not ready for therapy and may not accept it even if offered. They may be too impulsive and disorganized to attend specialized programs. This problem also arises in addiction clinics, where patients can remain in a "pre-contemplation" phase. In other words, patients have a general sense they have a problem, but are not ready to change, no matter what other people say. In such cases, it is best to keep the door open and wait until a patient is psychologically prepared to engage in treatment.

Finally, not all PD patients need specialized treatment. Even the much-maligned control comparison of treatment as usual (TAU) can also be effective, as shown by a meta-analysis (Finch et al, 2019). Supportive therapy of this kind can be reserved for patients who are either less symptomatic or are chronically dysfunctional. One can also sort out less severe cases that can be managed in primary care settings from those that require more specialized care.

Conclusions

From a public health perspective, it is unfortunate that the mental health system has failed to come to grip with one of the most common problems seen in clinical practice. PDs are not listed in the Global Burden of Disease (GBD 2017; Global Burden of Disease Study: Disease and Injury Incidence and Prevalence Collaborators, 2018). If they were, given their community prevalence, they would likely rank high. Moreover, PD patients are often misunderstood and mistreated, or even disliked by clinicians (Chartonas et al, 2017). This problem is a major obstacle, and specific methods of therapy have only helped somewhat to address it. But the needs for treatment can be met, at least partially, by shortening therapy.

Finally, psychotherapy for PD patients is highly consistent with both a trait-based dimensional approach and with the retention of one useful category (BPD). It needs more advocacy and more research to get its message out.

Chapter 11

Epilogue

I will end this book by highlighting the main theoretical and clinical implications of personality research.

1 The Five Factor Model (FFM) has extensive empirical support, and is thus far the best way to describe personality trait profiles.
2 The FFM can usefully account for the risk of psychopathology, and is a strong predictor of mental and physical outcomes in life.
3 Formal personality assessment is not routine in clinical practice, but can add useful information to evaluations.
4 Personality emerges from gene–environment interactions, and can best be understood in an interactive biopsychosocial model.
5 Personality trait profiles underlie many mental disorders, and can provide an explanation of similar life events lead to a wide range of clinical outcomes.
6 Personality disorders are rooted in pathological traits which have been amplified by the environment. They can be diagnosed as dimensions, categories, or both.
7 There is good evidence that psychotherapy can be used to mange personality disorders.
8 Effective psychotherapy for PDs involves the modification of traits. Much of this work involves skills that can modulate neuroticism.
9 Psychotherapy for PD patients should generally be brief, active, and well structured.
10 Personality profiles can be a predictor of success and failure in therapy.

This book has been written to advise mental health clinicians of the importance of understanding, assessing, and changing personality trait profiles in clinical practice. It has shown that the problematic aspects of personality are not limited to patients with personality disorders, but to most of the people who come to us for help.

DOI: 10.4324/9781003519942-11

Further research should focus on several unanswered questions about the role of personality in clinical work.

1 Determining the biological basis of personality, and how it is shaped by genes and rooted in brain structure and connections.
2 Using gene–environment and biopsychosocial models to predict the outcome of mental disorders linked to personality profiles.
3 A better understanding of the interactions between traumatic life events and the risk for psychopathology.
4 Studies to examine more precisely how personality traits affect psychopathology.
5 Determining how personality traits lead to personality disorders, giving weight to multiple risk factors, as well as to factors that promote resilience.
6 Measuring the role of personality and its modification in successful psychotherapy.

The take-home message of this book is that personality traits can be a key factor in treating patients with a wide range of life problems and disorders. Working with traits adds an extra dimension to treating the patients we see.

References

Abdellaoui, A., Yengo, L., Verweij, K. J., & Visscher, P. M. (2023). 15 years of GWAS discovery: Realizing the promise. *The American Journal of Human Genetics, 110*(2), 179–194.

Abraham, C., Conner, M., Jones, F., & O'Connor, D. (2024). *Health Psychology.* Routledge.

Achenbach, T. M., Ivanova, M. Y., Rescorla, L. A., Turner, L. V., & Althoff, R. R. (2016). Internalizing/externalizing problems: Review and recommendations for clinical and research applications. *Journal of the American Academy of Child & Adolescent Psychiatry, 55*, 647–656.

Alizadeh, Z., Feizi, A., Rejali, M., Afshar, H., Keshteli, A. H., & Adibi, P. (2018). The predictive value of personality traits for psychological problems (stress, anxiety and depression): Results from a large population based study. *Journal of Epidemiology and Global Health, 8*(3), 124–133.

Allport, G. W. (1937). *Personality: A Psychological Interpretation.* Holt.

Alshamsi, A., Pianesi, F., Lepri, B., Pentland, A., & Rahwan, I. (2015). Beyond contagion: Reality mining reveals complex patterns of social influence. *PloS One, 10*(8), e0135740.

Aluja, A., Balada, F., Atitsogbe, K. A., Rossier, J., & García, L. F. (2024). Convergence of the dimensional assessment of personality pathology (DAPP-BQ) and the five-factor personality inventory for the international classification of diseases 11th edition (FFiCD) in the context of the five-factor model and personality disorders. *BMC Psychiatry, 24*(1), 386.

Amato, P. R., Booth, A. (1997). *A Generation at Risk: Growing Up in an Era of Family Upheaval.* Harvard University Press.

American Psychological Association (2015). APA Dictionary of Psychology (2nd ed.). Washington DC.

American Psychiatric Association. (2022). *Diagnostic and Statistical Manual of Mental Disorders* (5th ed, text revision.). American Psychiatric Publishing.

Amstadter, A. B., Myers, J. M., & Kendler, K. S. (2014). Psychiatric resilience: Longitudinal twin study. *British Journal of Psychiatry, 205*, 275–280.

Assary, E., Zavos, H. M., Krapohl, E., Keers, R., & Pluess, M. (2021). Genetic architecture of environmental sensitivity reflects multiple heritable components: A twin study with adolescents. *Molecular Psychiatry, 26*(9), 4896–4904.

Atherton, O. E., Robins, R. W., Rentfrow, P. J., & Lamb, M. E. (2014). Personality correlates of risky health outcomes: Findings from a large Internet study. *Journal of Research in Personality*, *50*, 56–60.

Ayoub, M., Gosling, S. D., Potter, J., Shanahan, M., & Roberts, B. W. (2018). The relations between parental socioeconomic status, personality, and life outcomes. *Social Psychological and Personality Science*, *9*(3), 338–352.

Bach, B., Hopwood, C. J., & Simonsen, E. (2024). *Practitioner's Guide to the Alternative Model for Personality Disorders*. Guilford.

Bach, B., & Simonsen, S. (2024). *ICD-11 Personality Disorders: A Clinician's Guide*. Hogrefe Publishing.

Bagby, R. M., Gralnick, T. M., Al-Dajani, N., & Uliaszek, A. A. (2016). The role of the five-factor model in personality assessment and treatment planning. *Clinical Psychology: Science and Practice*, *23*(4), 365–381.

Ball, J. S., & Links, P. S. (2009). Borderline personality disorder and childhood trauma: Evidence for a causal relationship. *Current Psychiatry Reports*, *11*, 63–68.

Bandelow, B., Reitt, M., Röver, C., Michaelis, S., Görlich, Y., & Wedekind, D. (2015). Efficacy of treatments for anxiety disorders: A meta-analysis. *International Clinical Psychopharmacology*, *30*(4), 183–192.

Barkow, J. H., Cosmides, L., & Tooby, J. (Eds.). (1992). *The Adapted Mind: Evolutionary Psychology and the Generation of Culture*. Oxford University Press.

Barlow, D. (2010). Negative effects from psychological treatments. *American Psychologist*, *65*, 13–20.

Barlow, D. H., Curreri, A. J., & Woodard, L. S. (2021). Neuroticism and disorders of emotion: A new synthesis. *Current Directions in Psychological Science*, *30*(5), 410–417.

Barlow, D. H., Harris, B. A., Eustis, E. H., & Farchione, T. J. (2020). The unified protocol for transdiagnostic treatment of emotional disorders. *World Psychiatry*, *19*(2), 245.

Barlow, D. H., Sauer-Zavala, S., Carl, J. R., Bullis, J. R., & Ellard, K. K. (2014). The nature, diagnosis, and treatment of neuroticism: Back to the future. *Clinical Psychological Science*, *2*(3), 344–365.

Bateman, A., & Fonagy, P. (2004). *Psychotherapy for Borderline Personality Disorder: Mentalization Based Treatment*. Oxford University Press.

Beck, A. T., Butler, A. C., Brown, G. K., Dahlsgaard, K. K., Newman, C. F., & Beck, J. S. (2001). Dysfunctional beliefs discriminate personality disorders. *Behaviour Research and Therapy*, *39*(10), 1213–1225.

Beck, A. T., Davis, D. D., & Freeman, A. (2015). *Cognitive Therapy of Personality Disorders* (3rd ed.). Guilford.

Belsky, J., Caspi, A., Arsenault, L., Bleidorn, W., Fonagy, P., Goodman, M., & Houts, R. (2012). Etiological features of borderline personality related characteristics in a birth cohort of 12-year-old children. *Development and Psychopathology*, *24*, 251–265.

Belsky, J., Caspi, A., Moffitt, T. E., & Poulton, R. (2020). *The Origins of You: How Childhood Shapes Later Life*. Harvard University Press.

Belsky, J., & Pluess, M. (2009). Beyond diathesis stress: Differential susceptibility to environmental influences. *Psychological Bulletin, 135*(6), 885.

Bhadoria, R., Webb, K., & Morgan, J. F. (2010). Treating eating disorders: A review of the evidence. *Evidence-Based Mental Health, 13*, 1–4.

Binks, C.A., Fenton, M., McCarthy, L., Lee, T., Adams, C.E., & Duggan, C. Psychological therapies for people with borderline personality disorder. *Cochrane Database of Systematic Reviews* 2006, *1*, CD005652

Biskin, R. S., Paris, J., Zelkowitz, P., Mills, D., Laporte, L., & Heath, N. (2021). Nonsuicidal self-injury in early adolescence as a predictor of borderline personality disorder in early adulthood. *Journal of Personality Disorders, 35*(5), 764–775.

Black, D. W. (2022). *Bad Boys, Bad Men 3rd edition: Confronting Antisocial Personality Disorder (Sociopathy)*. Oxford University Press.

Blaffer Hrdy, S. (2024). *Father Time: A Natural History of Men and Babies*. Princeton University Press.

Bleidorn, W., Kandler, C., & Caspi, A. (2014). The behavioural genetics of personality development in adulthood—Classic, contemporary, and future trends. *European Journal of Personality, 28*(3), 244–255.

Blum, K., Baron, D., Jalali, R., Modestino, E. J., Steinberg, B., Elman, I., ... & Gold, M. S. (2020). Polygenic and multi locus heritability of alcoholism: Novel therapeutic targets to overcome psychological deficits. *Journal of Systems and Integrative Neuroscience, 7*. https://doi.org/10.15761/jsin.1000240

Blum, N., St. John, D., & Pfohl, B. (2008). Systems Training for Emotional Predictability and Problem Solving (STEPPS) for outpatients with borderline personality disorder: A randomized controlled trial and 1-year follow-up. *American Journal of Psychiatry, 165*, 468–478.

Bolton, D. (2023). A revitalized biopsychosocial model: Core theory, research paradigms, and clinical implications. *Psychological Medicine, 53*(16), 7504–7511.

Bolton, D., & Gillett, G. (2019). The biopsychosocial model 40 years on. In D. Bolton, & G. Gillett (Eds.), *The Biopsychosocial Model of Health and Disease: New Philosophical and Scientific Developments* (pp. 1–43). Palgrave Macmillan.

Boone, K., Choi-Kain, L., & Sharp, C. (2025). The relevance of generalist approaches to early intervention for personality disorder. *American Journal of Psychotherapy, 78*(1), 16–23.

Bornovalova, M. A., Hicks, B. M., Iacono, I., & McGue, M. (2009). Stability, change, and heritability of borderline personality disorder traits from adolescence to adulthood: A longitudinal twin study. *Development and Psychopathology, 21*, 1335–1353.

Bowlby, J. (1979). The Bowlby-Ainsworth attachment theory. *Behavioral and Brain Sciences, 2*(4), 637–638.

Boyle, G. J., Stern, Y., Stein, D. J., & Golden, C. L. (2020). *The SAGE Handbook of Clinical Neuropsychology: Clinical Neuropsychological Assessment and Diagnosis*. Sage.

Bracken, P., Thomas, P., & Timimi, S. (2012). Psychiatry beyond the current paradigm. *British Journal of Psychiatry, 201*, 430–434.

Brezo, J., Paris, J., & Turecki, G. (2006). Personality traits as correlates of suicidal ideation, suicide attempts, and suicide completions: A systematic review. *Acta Psychiatrica Scandinavica*, 113(3), 180–206.

Bschor, T., & Kilarski, L. L. (2016). Are antidepressants effective? A debate on their efficacy for the treatment of major depression in adults. *Expert Review of Neurotherapeutics*, 16(4), 367–374

Bucher, M. A., Suzuki, T., & Samuel, D. B. (2019). A meta-analytic review of personality traits and their associations with mental health treatment outcomes. *Clinical Psychology Review*, 70, 51–63.

Buss, D. A. (2024). *Evolutionary Psychology: The New Science of the Mind* (7th edition). Routledge.

Campbell, A. (2020). *A Mind of Her Own: The Evolutionary Psychology of Women* (2nd edition). Oxford University Press.

Carpenter, R. W., Tomko, R. L., Trull, T. J., & Boomsma, D. I. (2013). Gene-environment studies and borderline personality disorder: A review. *Current Psychiatry Reports*, 15, 336.

Caspi, A., McClay, J., Moffitt, T. E., Mill, J., Martin, J., Craig, I. W., ... & Poulton, R. (2002). Role of genotype in the cycle of violence in maltreated children. *Science*, 297(5582), 851–854.

Caspi, A., Sugden, K., Moffitt, T. E., Taylor, A., Craig, I. W., Harrington, H., et al. (2003). Influence of life stress on depression: Moderation by a polymorphism in the 5-HTT gene. *Science, 301,* 386–389.

Castle, D., Bosanac, P., & Rossell, S. (2015). Treating OCD: What to do when first-line therapies fail. *Australasian Psychiatry*, 23(4), 350–353.

Cattell, H. E., & Mead, A. D. (2008). The sixteen personality factor questionnaire (16PF). *The SAGE Handbook of Personality Theory and Assessment, 2,* 135–159.

Chartonas, D., Kyratsous, M., Dracass, S., Lee, T., & Bhui, K. (2017). Personality disorder: Still the patients that psychiatrists dislike? *BJPsych Bulletin*, 41, 12–17.

Chinneck, A., Thompson, K., Dobson, K. S., Stuart, H., Teehan, M., Stewart, S. H., & Team The Caring Campus. (2018). Neurotic personality traits and risk for adverse alcohol outcomes: Chained mediation through emotional disorder symptoms and drinking to cope. *Substance Use & Misuse*, 53(10), 1730–1741.

Chmielewski, M., Bagby, R. M., Markon, K., Ring, A. J., & Ryder, A. G. (2014). Openness to experience, intellect, schizotypal personality disorder, and psychoticism: Resolving the controversy. *Journal of Personality Disorders*, 28(4), 483–499.

Cicchetti, D., & Rogosch, F. A. (1996). Equifinality and multifinality in developmental psychopathology. *Development and Psychopathology*, 8(4), 597–600.

Clark, L. A. (2007). Assessment and diagnosis of personality disorder: Perennial issues and an emerging reconceptualization. *Annual Review of Psychology*, 58, 227–257.

Clark, L. A., Corona-Espinosa, A., Khoo, S., Kotelnikova, Y., Levin-Aspenson, H. F., Serapio-García, G., & Watson, D. (2021). Preliminary scales for ICD-11 personality disorder: Self and interpersonal dysfunction plus five personality disorder trait domains. *Frontiers in Psychology*, 12, 668724.

Clarke, D. M. (2018). Realizing the mass public benefit of evidence-based psychological therapies: The IAPT program. *Annual Review of Clinical Psychology, 10*. https://doi.org/10.1146/annurev-clinpsy-050817-084833

Cloninger, C. R., Svrakic, D. M., & Pryzbeck, T. R. (1993). A psychobiological model of temperament and character. *Archives of General Psychiatry, 50*, 975–990.

Cockerham, W. C. (2017). *Medical sociology*. Routledge.

Cockerham, W. C. (2020). *Sociology of Mental Disorder*. Routledge.

Cohen, P., & Cohen, J. (1984). The clinician's illusion. *Archives of General Psychiatry, 41*(12), 1178–1182.

Cohen, P., Crawford, T. N., Johnson, J. G., & Kasen, S. (2005). The children in the community study of developmental course of personality disorder. *Journal of Personality Disorders, 19*, 466–486.

Collishaw, S., Dunn, J., O'Connnor, T. G., Golding, J. (2007b). Avon Longitudinal Study of Parents and Children Study Team: Maternal childhood abuse and offspring adjustment over time. *Development and Psychopathology, 19*, 367–383.

Collishaw, S., Pickles, A., Messer, J., Rutter, M., Shearer, C., & Maughan, B. (2007a). Resilience to adult psychopathology following childhood maltreatment: Evidence from a community sample. *Child Abuse & Neglect, 31*(3), 211–229.

Corpas, J., Moriana, J. A., Venceslá, J. F., & Gálvez-Lara, M. (2021). Brief psychological therapies for emotional disorders in primary care: A systematic review and meta-analysis. *Clinical Psychology: Science and Practice, 28,* 363–376.

Corr, P. J., & Matthews, G. (Eds.). (2020). *The Cambridge Handbook of Personality Psychology* (2nd edition). Cambridge University Press.

Corrigan, P. W., & Watson, A. C. (2002). Understanding the impact of stigma on people with mental illness. *World Psychiatry, 1*, 16–20.

Crego, C., & Widiger, T. A. (2020). The convergent, discriminant, and structural relationship of the DAPP-BQ and SNAP with the ICD-11, DSM-5, and FFM trait models. *Psychological Assessment, 32*(1), 18–28.

Cristea, I. A., Gentilla, C., Cotet, C. D., Palomba, D., Barbui, C., & Cuijpers, P. (2017). Efficacy of psychotherapies for Borderline Personality Disorder: A systematic review and meta-analysis. *JAMA Psychiatry, 74*, 319–328.

Crowell, S. E., Beauchaine, T. P., & Linehan, M. M. (2009). A biosocial developmental model of borderline personality: Elaborating and extending Linehan's theory. *Psychological Bulletin, 135*(3), 495–510.

Cumming, G., Fidler, F., Kalinowski, P., & Lai, J. (2012). The statistical recommendations of the American Psychological Association Publication Manual: Effect sizes, confidence intervals, and meta-analysis. *Australian Journal of Psychology, 64*(3), 138–146.

Danayan, K., Newman, J., Benitah, K. *et al.* (2024). The impact of comorbid cluster B traits and personality disorders on depression treatment outcome: a systematic review and meta-analysis. *Nat. Mental Health* 2, 1392–1407

Davidson, K., Norrie, J., Tyrer, P., Gumley, A., Tata, P., Murray, H., & Palmer, S. (2006). The effectiveness of cognitive behavior therapy for borderline personality disorder: Results from the borderline personality disorder study of cognitive therapy (BOSCOT) trial. *Journal of Personality Disorders, 20*, 450–465.

DeRubeis, R. J., Siegle, G. J., & Hollon, S. D. (2088) Cognitive therapy versus medication for depression: Treatment outcomes and neural mechanisms. *Nature Reviews Neuroscience, 9,* 788–796.

DeYoung, C. G., & Allen, T. A. (2019). Personality neuroscience. In D. P. McAdams, R. L. Shiner, & J. Tackett (Eds.), *Handbook of Personality Development* (pp. 79–105). Guilford.

DeYoung, C. G., Beaty, R. E., Genç, E., Latzman, R. D., Passamonti, L., Servaas, M. N., Shackman, A. J., Smillie, L. D., Spreng, R. N., Viding, E., & Wacker, J. (2022). Personality neuroscience: An emerging field with bright prospects. *Personality Science, 3,* e7269. https://doi.org/10.5964/ps.7269

DeYoung, C. G., Hirsh, J. B., Shane, M. S., Papademetris, X., Rajeevan, N., & Gray, J. R. (2010). Testing predictions from personality neuroscience: Brain structure and the Big Five. *Psychological Science, 21*(6), 820–828.

Distel, M. A., Middeldorp, C. M., Trull, T. J., Derom, C. A., Willemsen, G., & Boomsma, D. I. (2011). Life events and borderline personality features: The influence of gene–environment interaction and gene–environment correlation. *Psychological Medicine, 41,* 849–860.

Dunner, D. L. (1992). Differential diagnosis of bipolar disorder. *Journal of Clinical Psychopharmacology, 12*(1), 7S–12S.

Durkheim, E. (1951). *Suicide: A study in sociology.* Trans. J. A. Spaulding, & G. Simpson. Free Press.

Eeles, J., & Walker, D. M. (2022). Mindfulness as taught in dialectical behaviour therapy: A scoping review. *Clinical Psychology & Psychotherapy, 29*(6), 1843–1853.

Ellis, B. J., & Boyce, W. T. (2008). Biological sensitivity to context. *Current Directions in Psychological Science, 17,* 183–186.

Engel, G. L. (1980). The clinical application of the biopsychosocial model. *American Journal of Psychiatry, 137,* 535–544.

Erkoreka, L., Zumarraga, M., Arrue, A., Zamalloa, M. I., Arnaiz, A., Olivas, O., Moreno-Calle, T., Saez, E., Garcia, J., Marin, E., Varela, N., Gonzalez-Pinto, A., & Basterreche, N. (2021). Genetics of adult attachment: An updated review of the literature. *World Journal of Psychiatry, 19*(11), 530–542.

Exner, J. E., Jr. (2003). *The Rorschach: A Comprehensive System* (4th edition). John Wiley & Sons Inc.

Eysenck, H. J. (1952). The organization of personality.

Feher, A., & Vernon, P. A. (2021). Looking beyond the Big Five: A selective review of alternatives to the Big Five model of personality. *Personality and Individual Differences, 169,* 110002.

Fergusson, D. M., Horwood, L. J., Miller, A. L., & Kennedy, M. A. (2011). Life stress, 5-HTTLPR and mental disorder: Findings from a 30-year longitudinal study. *The British Journal of Psychiatry, 198,* 129–135.

Fergusson, D. M., & Mullen, P. E. (1999). *Childhood Sexual Abuse: An Evidence Based Perspective.* Sage Publications.

Finch, E., Iliakis, E., Masland, S., & Choi-Kain, L. (2019). A meta-analysis of treatment as usual for borderline personality disorder. *Personality Disorders, 10,* 491–499.

Fink, L. A., Bernstein, D., Handelsman, L., Foote, J., & Lovejoy, M. (1995). Initial reliability and validity of the Childhood Trauma Interview: A new multidimensional measure of childhood interpersonal trauma. *American Journal of Psychiatry, 152*, 1329–1335.

Finzi-Dottan, R., & Karu, T. (2006). From emotional abuse in childhood to psychopathology in adulthood: A path mediated by immature defense mechanisms and self-esteem. *Journal of Nervous and Mental Disease, 194*, 616–621.

Fisher, S., & Greenberg, R. P. (1996). *Freud scientifically reappraised: Testing the theories and therapy.* New York.

Fleury, M. J., Djouini, A., Huỳnh, C., Tremblay, J., Ferland, F., Ménard, J. M., & Belleville, G. (2016). Remission from substance use disorders: A systematic review and meta-analysis. *Drug and Alcohol Dependence, 168*, 293–306.

Fodstad, E. C., Ushakova, A., Pallesen, S., Hagen, E., Erga, A. H., & Erevik, E. K. (2022). Personality and substance use disorder: Characteristics as measured by NEO-personality inventory–revised. *Frontiers in Psychology, 13*, 982763.

Fok, M. L. Y., Hayes, R. D., Chang, C. K., Stewart, R., Callard, F. J., & Moran, P. (2012). Life expectancy at birth and all-cause mortality among people with personality disorder. *Journal of Psychosomatic Research, 73*(2), 104–107.

Fossati, A., Maddeddu, F., & Maffei, C. (1999). Borderline personality disorder and childhood sexual abuse: A metanalytic study. *Journal of Personality Disorders, 13*, 268–280.

Frances, A. (2013). *Losing Normal.* Morrow.

Frandsen, F. W., Simonsen, S., Poulsen, S., Sørensen, P., & Lau, M. E. (2020). Social anxiety disorder and avoidant personality disorder from an interpersonal perspective. *Psychology and Psychotherapy: Theory, Research and Practice, 93*(1), 88–104.

Freeman, D. (1999). *The Fateful Hoaxing of Margaret Mead: A Historical Analysis of Her Samoan Research* (p. 208). Westview Press.

French, L. R. M., Turner, K. M., Dawson, S., & Moran, P. (2017). Psychological treatment of depression and anxiety in patients with co-morbid personality disorder: A scoping study of trial evidence. *Personality and Mental Health, 11*(2), 101–117.

Freud, S. (1937/1962). Analysis terminable and interminable. In James Stracey, Anna Freud, & Angela Richards (Eds.), *The Standard Edition of the Psychological Works of Sigmund Freud* (Vol. 23, pp. 216–254). Hogarth Press.

Friedman, H. S., Tucker, J. S., Schwartz, J. E., Martin, L. R., Tomlinson-Keasey, C., Wingard, D. L., & Criqui, M. H. (1995). Childhood conscientiousness and longevity: Health behaviors and cause of death. *Journal of Personality and Social Psychology, 68*(4), 696–703.

Friedman, M., & Rosenman, R. (2020). How to tell a Type A from a Type B. In Stewart L. Tubbs (Ed.), *Shared Experiences in Human Communication* (pp. 124–129). Routledge.

Fruhbauerova, M., Stumpp, N., & Sauer-Zavala, S. (2024). The utility of the Unified Protocol in treating borderline features. *Journal of Psychopathology and Behavioral Assessment, 46*(1), 137–146.

Furedi, F. (2002). *Paranoid Parenting: Why Ignoring the Experts May Be Best for Your Child*. Review Press.

Furedi, F. (2017). *Therapeutic Culture*. Routledge.

Gale, C. R., Booth, T., Mõttus, R., Kuh, D., & Deary, I. J. (2013). Neuroticism and extraversion in youth predict mental wellbeing and life satisfaction 40 years later. *Journal of Research in Personality*, 47(6), 687–697.

Garcia, D. (2024). The big, the dark, and the biopsychosocial shades of harmony: personality traits and harmony in life. *Behavioral Sciences*, 14(10), 873.

Gelernter, J. (2015). Genetics of complex traits in psychiatry. *Biological Psychiatry*, 77(1), 36–42.

Ghaemi, S. N. (2009). The rise and fall of the biopsychosocial model. *British Journal of Psychiatry*, 195(1), 3–4.

Giesen-Bloo, J., Van Dyck, R., Spinhoven, P., Van Tilburg, W., Dirksen, C., Van Asselt, T., ... & Arntz, A. (2006). Outpatient psychotherapy for borderline personality disorder: Randomized trial of schema-focused therapy vs transference-focused psychotherapy. *Archives of General Psychiatry*, 63, 649–658.

Global Burden of Disease Study: Disease and Injury Incidence and Prevalence Collaborators. (2018). Global, regional, and national incidence, prevalence, and years lived with disability for 354 diseases and injuries for 195 countries and territories, 1990–2017: A systematic analysis for the Global Burden of Disease Study 2017. *Lancet*, 392, 1789–1858.

Gluschkoff, K., Jokela, M., & Rosenström, T. (2021). General psychopathology factor and borderline personality disorder: Evidence for substantial overlap from two nationally representative surveys of US adults. *Personality Disorders: Theory, Research, and Treatment*, 12(1), 86.

Glymour, M. M., Avendano, M., & Kawachi, I. (2014). Socioeconomic status and health. *Social Epidemiology*, 2, 17–63.

Gold, I. (2009). Reduction in psychiatry. *The Canadian Journal of Psychiatry*, 54(8), 506–512.

Goldberg, L. R. (1990). An alternative "description of personality": The Big-Five factor structure. *Journal of Personality and Social Psychology*, 59(6), 1216–1229.

Goldstein, S., & Brooks, R. (eds.) (2012). *Handbook of Resilience in Children*. Springer.

Gore, W. L., & Pincus, A. L. (2013). Dependency and the five-factor model. In T. A. Widiger & P. T. Costa, Jr. (Eds.), *Personality Disorders and The Five-Factor Model of Personality* (3rd ed., pp. 163–177). American Psychological Association.

Granneman, J. (2017). *The Secret Lives of Introverts: Inside Our Hidden World*. Simon and Schuster.

Grant, B. F., Chou, S. P., Saha, T. D., Pickering, R. P., Kerridge, B. T., Ruan, W. J., ... & Hasin, D. S. (2017). Prevalence of 12-month alcohol use, high-risk drinking, and DSM-IV alcohol use disorder in the United States, 2001–2002 to 2012–2013: Results from the National Epidemiologic Survey on Alcohol and Related Conditions. *JAMA Psychiatry*, 74(9), 911–923.

Gratzer, D., & Goldbloom, D. (2016). Making evidence-based psychotherapy more accessible in Canada. *The Candian Journal of Psychiatry, 51,* 618–623.

Gunderson, J. G., Stout, R. L., McGlashan, T. H., Shea, T., Morey, L. C., Grilo, C. M., Zanarini, M. C., Yen, S., Markowitz, J. C., Sanislow, C., Ansell, E., Pinto, A., & Skodol, A. E. (2011). Ten-year course of Borderline Personality Disorder: Psychopathology and function from the collaborative longitudinal personality disorders study. *Archives of General Psychiatry, 68,* 827–837.

Guzder, J., Paris, J., Zelkowitz, P., & Marchessault, K. (1996). Risk factors for borderline pathology in children. *Journal of the American Academy of Child Adolescent Psychiatry, 35,* 26–33.

Haberstick, B. C., Boardman, J. D., Wagner, B., Smolen, A., Hewitt, J. K., Killeya-Jones, L. A., & Mullan Harris, K. (2016). Depression, stressful life events, and the impact of variation in the serotonin transporter: Findings from the National Longitudinal Study of Adolescent to Adult Health (Add Health). *PLoS One, 11*(3), e0148373.

Haidt, J. (2024). *The Anxious Generation: How the Great Rewiring of Childhood is Causing an Epidemic of Mental Illness.* Random House.

Haidt, J., Graham, J., & Joseph, C. (2009). Above and below left–right: Ideological narratives and moral foundations. *Psychological Inquiry, 20*(2–3), 110–119.

Hare, R. D. (2020). The PCL-R assessment of psychopathy. In A. Felthous, & H. Sass (Eds.), *The Wiley International Handbook on Psychopathic Disorders and the Law* (pp. 63–106). John Wiley.

Harkness, A. R., & Lilienfeld, S. O. (1997). Individual differences science for treatment planning: Personality traits *Psychological Assessment, 9,* 349–360.

Harris, J. R. (1997). *The Nurture Assumption: Why Children Turn Out the Way they Do.* Free Press.

Hartung, C. M., & Lefler, E. K. (2019). Sex and gender in psychopathology: *DSM–5* and beyond. *Psychological Bulletin, 145*(4), 390–409.

Haslam, N. (2016). Concept creep: Psychology's expanding concepts of harm and pathology. *Psychological inquiry, 27*(1), 1–17.

Hayes, S. C., & Hofmann, S. G. (2021). "Third-wave" cognitive and behavioral therapies and the emergence of a process-based approach to intervention in psychiatry. *World Psychiatry, 20*(3), 363–375.

Heilmayr, D., & Friedman, H. (2020). Personality and health. *Cambridge Handbook of Psychology, Health and Medicine.* Cambridge University Press.

Herman, J., & van der Kolk, B. (1987). Traumatic antecedents of borderline personality disorder. In B. van der Kolk (Ed.), *Psychological Trauma* (pp.111–126). American Psychiatric Press.

Hernandez, A., Arntz, A., & Gaviria, A. M. (2012). Relationships between childhood maltreatment, parenting style, and borderline personality disorder criteria. *Journal of Personality Disorders, 26,* 727–736.

Herpertz, S. C., Huprich, S. K., Bohus, M., Chanen, A., Goodman, M., Mehlum, L., ... & Sharp, C. (2017). The challenge of transforming the diagnostic system of personality disorders. *Journal of Personality Disorders, 31*(5), 577–589.

Hipwell, A., Chung, T., Stepp, S., & McTeague, K. (2010). The Pittsburgh girls study: Overview and initial findings. *Journal of Clinical Child & Adolescent Psychology, 39,* 506–521.

Hobson, J. A., & Leonard, J. A. (2001). *Out of its Mind: Psychiatry in Crisis—a Call for Reform*. Perseus Publishing.

Hong, R. Y., & Tan, Y. L. (2021). DSM-5 personality traits and cognitive risks for depression, anxiety, and obsessive-compulsive symptoms. *Personality and Individual Differences, 169*, 110041.

Hopwood, C. J. (2018). A framework for treating DSM-5 alternative model for personality disorder features. *Personality and Mental Health, 12*(2), 107–125.

Hopwood, C. J., Bagby, R. M., Gralnick, T., Ro, E., Ruggero, C., Mullins-Sweatt, S., ... & Zimmermann, J. (2020). Integrating psychotherapy with the hierarchical taxonomy of psychopathology (HiTOP). *Journal of Psychotherapy Integration, 30*(4), 477.

Horwitz, L. (1974). *Clinical Prediction in Psychotherapy*. Jason Aronson.

Horwitz, Allan V. (2021). *DSM: A history of psychiatry's bible*. JHU Press.

Huband, N., McMurran, M., Evans, C., & Duggan, C. (2007). Social problem-solving plus psychoeducation for adults with personality disorder: Pragmatic randomised controlled trial. *British Journal of Psychiatry, 190*, 307–313.

Inbar, Y., & Lammers, J. (2012). Political diversity in social and personality psychology. *Perspectives on Psychological Science, 7*(5), 496–503.

Inglehart, R. (2020). *Modernization and Postmodernization: Cultural, Economic, and Political Change in 43 Societies*. Princeton University Press.

Insel, T. R., & Quirion, R. (2005). Psychiatry as a clinical neuroscience discipline. *JAMA, 294*(17), 2221–2224.

Jakubczyk, A., Trucco, E. M., Kopera, M., Kobyliński, P., Suszek, H., Fudalej, S., ... & Wojnar, M. (2018). The association between impulsivity, emotion regulation, and symptoms of alcohol use disorder. *Journal of Substance Abuse Treatment, 91*, 49–56.

James, W. (1890). *The Principles of Psychology*. Taylor and Francis.

Jang, K. L. (2005). *The Behavioral Genetics of Psychopathology: A Clinical Guide*. Routledge.

Jarvi, S., Jackson, B., Swenson, L., & Crawford, H. (2013). The impact of social contagion on non-suicidal self-injury: A review of the literature. *Archives of Suicide Research, 17*(1), 1–19.

Johnson, B. T., & Acabchuk, R. L. (2018). What are the keys to a longer, happier life? Answers from five decades of health psychology research. *Social Science & Medicine, 196*, 218–226.

Johnson, J. J., Cohen, P., Brown, J., Smailes, E. M., & Bernstein, D. P. (1999). Childhood maltreatment increases risk for personality disorders during early adulthood. *Archives of General Psychiatry, 56*, 600–606.

Jones, D. N., & Paulhus, D. L. (2014). Introducing the Short Dark Triad (SD3): A brief measure of dark personality traits. *Assessment, 21*(1), 28–41.

Kagan, J. (1998a). *Galen's Prophecy: Temperament in Human Nature*. Routledge.

Kagan, J. (1998b). A parent's influence is peerless. *Boston Globe*. September 13.

Kajonius, P., & Mac Giolla, E. (2017). Personality traits across countries: Support for similarities rather than differences. *PloS One, 12*(6), e0179646.

Kalin, N. H. (2020). The critical relationship between anxiety and depression. *American Journal of Psychiatry, 177*(5), 365–367.

Kajonius, P. J. (2017). The short personality inventory for DSM-5 and its conjoined structure with the common five-factor model. *International Journal of Testing, 17*(4), 372–384.

Kendler, K. S., Ohlsson, H., Sundquist, K., & Sundquist, J. (2018). Sources of parent-offspring resemblance for major depression in a national Swedish extended adoption study. *JAMA Psychiatry, 75*(2), 194–200.

Kennedy, E. (2013). Orchids and dandelions: How some children are more susceptible to environmental influences for better or worse and the implications for child development. *Clinical Child Psychology and Psychiatry, 18*, 319–321.

Kern, M. L., & Friedman, H. S. (2015). *Health Psychology.* Oxford University Press.

Kessler, R. C., Aguilar-Gaxiola, S., Alonso, J., Chatterji, S., Lee, S., Ormel, J., ... & Wang, P. S. (2009). The global burden of mental disorders: an update from the WHO World Mental Health (WMH) surveys. *Epidemiology and psychiatric sciences, 18*(1), 23–33.

Kirkland, J. M., Edgar, E. L., Patel, I., Feustel, P., Belin, S., & Kopec, A. M. (2024). Synaptic pruning during adolescence shapes adult social behavior in both males and females. *Developmental Psychobiology, 66*(3), e22473.

Kitayama, S., & Salvador, C. E. (2024). Cultural psychology: Beyond east and west. *Annual Review of Psychology, 75*, 495–526.

Klein, D. N., Kotov, R., & Bufferd, S. J. (2011). Personality and depression: Explanatory models and review of the evidence. *Annual Review of Clinical Psychology, 7*, 269–295.

Klonsky, E. D., & Meyer, A. (2008). Childhood sexual abuse and non-suicidal self-injury: meta-analysis. *British Journal of Psychiatry, 192*, 166–170.

Kofman, Y. B., Selbe, S., Szentkúti, P., Horváth-Puhó, E., Rosellini, A. J., Lash, T. L., ... & Sumner, J. A. (2024). Sex differences in psychopathology following potentially traumatic experiences. *JAMA Network Open, 7*(2), e240201–e24020.

Kolla, N. J., & Vinette, S. A. (2017). Monoamine oxidase a in antisocial personality disorder and borderline personality disorder. *Current Behavioral Neuroscience Reports, 4*, 41–48.

Kowalski, C. M., Vernon, P. A., & Schermer, J. A. (2021). The Dark Triad and facets of personality. *Current Psychology, 40*, 5547–5558.

Kramer, U. (2020). Individualizing psychotherapy research designs. *Journal of Psychotherapy Integration, 30*(3), 440–457.

Kramer, U., Beuchat, H., Grandjean, L., & Pascual-Leone, A. (2020). How personality disorders change in psychotherapy: A concise review of process. *Current Psychiatry Reports, 22*, 1–9.

Krueger, R. F., & Hobbs, K. A. (2020). An overview of the DSM-5 alternative model of personality disorders. *Psychopathology, 53*(3–4), 126–132.

Kupper, N., & Denollet, J. (2018). Type D personality as a risk factor in coronary heart disease: A review of current evidence. *Current Cardiology Reports, 20*, 1–8.

Lambert, M. (2007). What we have learned from a decade of research aimed at improving psychotherapy outcome in routine care. *Psychotherapy Research, 17*, 1–14.

Lampropoulos, G. K. (2011). Failure in psychotherapy: An introduction. *Journal of Clinical Psychology, 67*(11), 1093–1095.

Laporte, L., & Guttman, H. (1996). Traumatic childhood experiences as risk factors for borderline and other personality disorders. *Journal of Personality Disorders, 10*, 247–259.

Laporte, L., Paris, J., Russell, J., & Guttman, H. (2011). Psychopathology, trauma, and personality traits in patients with borderline personality disorder and their sisters. *Journal of Personality Disorders, 25*, 448, 462.

Laporte, L., Paris, J., Russell, J., Guttman, H., & Correa, J. (2013). Childhood trauma in patients with borderline personality disorder and their sisters. *Child Maltreatment, 17*(4), 318–329.

Laporte, L., Paris, J., Zelkowitz, P., & Cardin, J. F. (2018). Clinical outcomes of stepped care for the treatment of borderline personality disorder. *Personality and Mental Health, 12*, 49–58.

Lazar, S. G. (2014). The cost-effectiveness of psychotherapy for the major psychiatric diagnoses. *Psychodynamic Psychiatry, 42*, 423–457.

Lebel, C., & Beaulieu, C. (2011). Longitudinal development of human brain wiring continues from childhood into adulthood. *Journal of neuroscience, 31*(30), 10937–10947.

Leichsenring, F., & Rabung, S. (2008). Effectiveness of long-term psychodynamic psychotherapy: A meta-analysis. *JAMA, 300*, 1551–1556.

Leichsenring, F., Rabung, S., & Leibing, E. (2004). The efficacy of short-term psychodynamic psychotherapy in specific psychiatric disorders: A meta-analysis. *Archives of General Psychiatry, 61*, 1208–1216.

Levitt, E. E., & Gotts, E. E. (2021). *The Clinical Application of MMPI Special Scales*. Routledge.

Lewis, D., Al-Shawaf, L., & Buss, D. (2020). Evolutionary personality psychology. In P. J. Corr & G. Matthews (Ed.), *The Cambridge Handbook of Personality Psychology* (pp. 223–234). Cambridge Press.

Lewis, K. L., & Grenyer, B. F. S. (2009). Borderline personality or complex post-traumatic stress disorder? An update on the controversy. *Harvard Review of Psychiatry, 17*, 322–328.

Lilienfeld, S. O., Wood, J. M., & Garb, H. N. (2000). The scientific status of projective techniques. *Psychological Science in the Public Interest*, 27–66.

Linehan, M. M. (2014). *DBT Skills Training Manual* (Second Edition). Guilford.

Litchfield, C. A., Quinton, G., Tindle, H., Chiera, B., Kikillus, K. H., & Roetman, P. (2017). The 'Feline Five': An exploration of personality in pet cats (Felis catus). *PloS One, 12*(8), e0183455.

Livesley, W. J., Jang, K.L., & Vernon, P. A. (1998). Phenotypic and genetic structure of traits delineating personality disorder. *Archives of General Psychiatry, 55*(10), 941–948.

Longley, S. L., & Gleiser, T. S. (2023). Efficacy of the Unified Protocol: A systematic review and meta-analysis of randomized controlled trials. *Clinical Psychology: Science and Practice, 30*(2), 208–221.

Luecken, L. J., & Roubinov, D. S. (2012). Health following childhood parental death. *Social and Personality Psychology Compass, 6*, 243–257.

Lungu, A., & Linehan, M. M. (2016). Dialectical behavior therapy: A comprehensive multi- and transdiagnostic intervention. *The Oxford Handbook of Cognitive and Behavioral Therapies* (pp. 200–214). Oxford University Press.

Luo, J., Zhang, B., Cao, M., & Roberts, B. W. (2022). The stressful personality: A meta-analytical review of the relation between personality and stress. *Personality and Social Psychology Review, 27*(2), 128–194.

Lynam, D. R., & Miller, J. D. (2019). The basic trait of antagonism: An unfortunately underappreciated construct. *Journal of Research in Personality, 81*, 118–126.

Lynch, T. R. (2018). *Radically Open Dialectical Behavior Therapy: Theory and Practice for Treating Disorders of Overcontrol*. New Harbinger Publications.

Lynch, T. R., Hempel, R. J., & Dunkley, C. (2015). Radically open-dialectical behavior therapy for disorders of over-control: Signaling matters. *American Journal of Psychotherapy, 69*(2), 141–162.

MacKenzie, K. R. (1996). The time-limited psychotherapies: An overview. *American Psychiatric Press Review of Psychiatry, 15*, 11–21.

Malinovsky-Rummell, R., & Hansen, D.J. (1993). Long-term consequences of physical abuse. *Psychological Bulletin, 114*, 68–79.

Marceau, E. M., Meuldijk, D., Townsend, M. L., Solowij, N., & Grenyer, B. F. (2018). Biomarker correlates of psychotherapy outcomes in borderline personality disorder: A systematic review. *Neuroscience & Biobehavioral Reviews, 94*, 166–178.

Marks, D. F., Murray, M., Locke, A., Annunziato, R. A., & Estacio, E. V. (2024). *Health Psychology: Theory, Research and Practice*. Sage.

Marrero-Quevedo, R. J., Blanco-Hernández, P. J., & Hernández-Cabrera, J. A. (2019). Adult attachment and psychological well-being: The mediating role of personality. *Journal of Adult Developent, 26*, 41–56.

Masten, A. S., & Cicchetti, D. (2016). Resilience in development: Progress and transformation. *Developmental Psychopathology, 4*(3), 271–333.

Maxwell, K., Donnellan, M. B., Hopwood, C. J., & Ackerman, R. A. (2011). The two faces of Narcissus? An empirical comparison of the Narcissistic Personality Inventory and the Pathological Narcissism Inventory. *Personality and Individual Differences, 50*(5), 577–582.

McAdams, D. P. (2021). Narrative identity and the life story. *Handbook of Personality: Theory and Research*, 122–141.

McCrae, R. R., & Costa, P. T., (2010). *NEO Inventories: Professional Manual*. Psychological Assessment Resources, Inc.

McCrae, R. R., & Costa, P. T., Jr. (2013). Introduction to the empirical and theoretical status of the five-factor model of personality traits. In T. A. Widiger & P. T. Costa, Jr. (Eds.), *Personality Disorders and the Five-Factor Model of Personality* (3rd ed., pp. 15–27). American Psychological Association.

McCrae, R. R., & Terracciano, A. (2015). The Five-Factor Model and its correlates in individuals and cultures. In F. J. R. Van de Vijver, D. A. Van Hemert, & Y. H. Poortinga (Eds.), *Multilevel Analysis of Individuals and Cultures* (pp. 249–283). Psychology Press.

McCrae, R. R., Costa, P. T., Jr., Ostendorf, F., Angleitner, A., et al (2000). Nature over nurture: Temperament, personality, and life span development. *Journal of Personality and Social Psychology, 78*, 173–186.

McCrae, R. R., De Bolle, F., Löckenhoff, C. E., & Terracciano, S. (2021). Lifespan trait development: Toward an adequate theory of personality. In J. F. Rauthmann

(Ed.), *The Handbook of Personality Dynamics and Processes* (pp. 621–682). Academic Press.

McKay, M. T., Kilmartin, L., Meagher, A., Cannon, M., Healy, C., & Clarke, M. C. (2022). A revised and extended systematic review and meta-analysis of the relationship between childhood adversity and adult psychiatric disorder. *Journal of Psychiatric Research, 156,* 268–283.

McLaughlin, K. A., Green, M. J., Sampson, N. A., Zaslavsky, A. M., & Kessler, R. C. (2010). Childhood adversities and adult psychopathology in the National Comorbidity Survey Replication (NCS-R) III: Associations with functional impairment related to DSM-IV disorders *Psychological Medicine, 40,* 857–859.

McMain, S. F., Chapman, A. L., Kuo, J. R., Dixon-Gordon, K. L., Guimond, T. H., Labrish, C., ... & Streiner, D. L. (2022). The effectiveness of 6 versus 12 months of dialectical behavior therapy for borderline personality disorder: A noninferiority randomized clinical trial. *Psychotherapy and Psychosomatics, 91*(6), 382–397.

McMain, S. F., Links, P., Gnam, W. H., Guimond, T., Cardish, R. J., Korman, L., & Streiner, D. L. (2009). A randomized trial of dialectical behavior therapy versus general psychiatric management for borderline personality disorder. *American Journal of Psychiatry, 166,* 1365–1374.

McNally, R. J. (2003a). *Remembering Trauma.* Belknap Press/Harvard University Press.

McNally, R. J. (2023b). Post-traumatic stress disorder and dissociative disorders. In R. F. Krueger & P. H. Blaney (Eds.), *Oxford Textbook of Psychopathology* (pp. 199–227). Oxford University Press.

Messina, I., Grecucci, A., & Viviani, R. (2021). Neurobiological models of emotion regulation: A meta-analysis of neuroimaging studies of acceptance as an emotion regulation strategy. *Social Cognitive and Affective Neuroscience, 16*(3), 257–267.

Meuldijk, D., McCarthy, A., Bourke, M. E., & Grenyer, B. F. S. (2018). The value of psychological treatment for borderline personality disorder: Systematic review and cost offset analysis of economic evaluations. *Plus One. 12.* https://doi.org/10.1371/journal.pone.0171592

Miller, G. A. (1956). The magical number seven, plus or minus two. *Psychological Review, 63*(2), 81–97.

Miller, J. D., Lynam, D. R., Vize, C., Crowe, M., Sleep, C., Maples-Keller, J. L., ... & Campbell, W. K. (2018). Vulnerable narcissism is (mostly) a disorder of neuroticism. *Journal of Personality, 86*(2), 186–199.

Miller, W. R., & Rollnick, S. (2012). *Motivational Interviewing: Helping People Change.* Guilford.

Millon, T. (1993). Borderline personality disorder: A psychosocial epidemic. In J. Paris (Ed.), *Borderline Personality Disorder: Etiology and Treatment* (pp. 197–210). American Psychiatric Press.

Minarikova, K. B., Prasko, J., Holubova, M., Vanek, J., Kantor, K., Slepecky, M., ... & Ociskova, M. (2022). Hallucinations and other psychotic symptoms in patients with borderline personality disorder. *Neuropsychiatric Disease and Treatment, 18,* 787.

Mischel, W. (1968). *Personality and Assessment.* John Wiley.

Mitchell, K. (2018). *Innate: How the Wiring of Our Brains Shapes Who We Are*. Princeton University Press.

Moffitt, T. E. (2017). Adolescence-limited and life-course-persistent antisocial behavior: A developmental taxonomy. *Biosocial Theories of Crime*, 69–96.

Mols, F., & Denollet, J. (2010). Type D personality among noncardiovascular patient populations: A systematic review. *General Hospital Psychiatry*, 32(1), 66–72.

Moran, P. (1999). The epidemiology of antisocial personality disorder. *Social Psychiatry and Psychiatric Epidemiology*, 34, 231–242.

Moran, P., Coffey, C., Romaniuk, H., Olsson, C., Borschmann, R., Carlin, J. B., & Patton, G. C. (2012). The natural history of self-harm from adolescence to young adulthood: A population-based cohort study. *The Lancet*, 379(9812), 236–243.

Morgan, W. (2002). Origin and history of the earliest Thematic Apperception test. *Journal of Personality Assessment*, 79, 422–445.

Mulay, A. L., Waugh, M. H., Fillauer, J. P., Bender, D. S., Bram, A., Cain, N. M., ... & Skodol, A. E. (2019). Borderline personality disorder diagnosis in a new key. *Borderline Personality Disorder and Emotion Dysregulation*, 6, 1–16.

Murphy, S. A., Fisher, P. A., & Robie, C. (2021). International comparison of gender differences in the five-factor model of personality: An investigation across 105 countries. *Journal of Research in Personality*, 90, 104047.

Nagel, M., Jansen, P.R., Stringer, S. et al. (2018). Meta-analysis of genome-wide association studies for neuroticism in 449,484 individuals identifies novel genetic loci and pathways. *Nature Genetics*, 50, 920–927.

Nettle, D. (2005a). *Personality: What Makes You The Way You Are*. Oxford University Press.

Nettle, D. (2005b). An evolutionary approach to the extraversion continuum. *Evolution and Human Behavior*, 26(4), 363–373.

Nettle, D. (2009) *Personality: What makes you the way you are*. Oxford University Press

Newton-Howes, G., Tyrer, P., & Johnson, T. (2006). Personality disorder and the outcome of depression: Meta-analysis of published studies. *The British Journal of Psychiatry*, 188(1), 13–20.

Niven, K. (2022). Does interpersonal emotion regulation ability change with age? *Human Resource Management Review*, 32(20). http://dx.doi.org/10.1016/j.hrmr.2021.100847

Nygren, A., Reutfors, J., Brandt, L., Bodén, R., Nordenskjöld, A., & Tiger, M. (2023). Response to electroconvulsive therapy in treatment-resistant depression: nationwide observational follow-up study. *BJPsych Open*, 9(2), e35.

O'Connor, T. G., Croft, C., & Steele, H. (2000). The contributions of behavioural genetic studies to attachment theory. *Attachment & Human Development*, 2(1), 107–122.

O'Sullivan, M., Murphy, A., & Bourke, J. (2017). The cost of dialectic behaviour therapy (DBT) for people diagnosed with Borderline Personality Disorder (BPD): A review of the literature. *Value in Health*, 20, A714.

Oehler, A., & Wedlich, F. (2018). The relationship of extraversion and neuroticism with risk attitude, risk perception, and return expectations. *Journal of Neuroscience, Psychology, and Economics*, 11(2), 63–92.

Ogden, L. E. (2012). Do animals have personality? The importance of individual differences. *BioScience, 62*(6), 533–537.

Oliveira, P., & Fearon, P. (2019). The biological bases of attachment. *Adoption & Fostering, 43,* 274–293.

Öngür, D., & Paulus, M. P. (2024). Embracing complexity in psychiatry—From reductionistic to systems approaches. *The Lancet Psychiatry.*

Ormel, J., Hollon, S. D., Kessler, R. C., Cuijpers, P., & Monroe, S. M. (2022). More treatment but no less depression: The treatment-prevalence paradox. *Clinical Psychology Review, 91,* 102111.

Orth, U., Krauss, S., & Back, M. D. (2024). Development of narcissism across the life span: A meta-analytic review of longitudinal studies. *Psychological Bulletin, 150*(6), 643–655.

Oshio, A., Taku, K., Hirano, M., & Saeed, G. (2018). Resilience and Big Five personality traits: A meta-analysis. *Personality and Individual Differences, 127,* 54–60.

Oud, M., Arntz, A., Hermens, M. L., Verhoef, R., & Kendall, T. (2018). Specialized psychotherapies for adults with borderline personality disorder: A systematic review and meta-analysis. *Australian & New Zealand Journal of Psychiatry, 52,* 949–961.

Paris, J. (1998). *Working with Traits: Psychotherapy of Personality Disorders.* Jason Aronson.

Paris, J. (2010). Effectiveness of differing psychotherapy approaches in the treatment of borderline personality disorder. *Current Psychiatry Reports, 12,* 56–60.

Paris, J. (2015). *A Concise Guide to Personality Disorders.* American Psychological Association Publishing.

Paris, J. (2020a). *The Treatment of Borderline Personality Disorder; A Guide to Evidence-Based Practice* (2nd edition, revised and updated). Guilford Press.

Paris, J. (2020b). Access to psychotherapy for patients with personality disorders. *Personality and Mental Health, 14*(3), 246–253.

Paris, J. (2020c). *Overdiagnosis in Psychiatry* (2nd edition). Oxford University Press.

Paris, J. (2022a). *Myths of Trauma.* Oxford University Press.

Paris, J. (2022b). *Nature and Nurture in Personality and Psychopathology: A Guide for Clinicians.* Routledge.

Paris, J. (2024). *Half in Love with Death* (2nd edition). Routledge.

Paris, J. (2025). *A Concise Guide to Borderline Personality Disorder.* American Psychological Association Publishing.

Paris, J., & Zweig-Frank, H. (2001). A 27 year follow-up of patients with borderline personality disorder. *Comprehensive Psychiatry, 42,* 482–487.

Paris, J., Zweig-Frank, H., & Guzder, J. (1994a). Risk factors for borderline personality in male outpatients. *Journal of Nervous and Mental Disease, 182,* 375–380.

Paris, J., Zweig-Frank, H., & Guzder, J. (1994b). Psychological risk factors for borderline personality disorder in female patients. *Comprehensive Psychiatry, 35,* 301–305.

Parker, G. (2005). Beyond major depression. *Psychological Medicine, 35*(4), 467–474.

Paulhus, D. L., & Vazire, S. (2007). The self-report method. In R. Robins, C. Fraley, R. Krueger (Eds.), *Handbook of Research Methods in Personality Psychology* (pp. 224–239). Guilford.

Peters, E. M., John, A., Bowen, R., Baetz, M., & Balbuena, L. (2018). Neuroticism and suicide in a general population cohort: Results from the UK Biobank Project. *BJPsych Open*, 4(2), 62–68.

Picardi, A., Giuliani, E., & Gigantesco, A. (2020). Genes and environment in attachment. *Neuroscience & Biobehavioral Reviews*, 112, 254–269.

Pinker, S. (2009). *How the Mind Works* (2nd Edition). Norton.

Pinker, S. (2004). *The Blank Slate: The Modern Denial of Human Nature*. Viking.

Plomin, R. (2018). *Blueprint: How DNA Makes Us Who We Are*. Allen Lane.

Plomin, R. (2019). *Blueprint: How DNA makes us who we are*. MIT Press.

Pluess, M., Assary, E., Lionetti, F., Lester, K. J., Krapohl, E., Aron, E. N., & Aron, A. (2018). Environmental sensitivity in children: Development of the Highly Sensitive Child Scale and identification of sensitivity groups. *Developmental Psychology*, 54(1), 51.

Porter, C., Palmier-Claus, J., Branitsky, A., Mansell, W., Warwick, H., & Varese, F. (2020). Childhood adversity and borderline personality disorder: A meta-analysis. *Acta Psychiatrica Scandinavica*, 141(1), 6–20.

Rector, N. A., Bagby, R. M., Huta, V., & Ayearst, L. E. (2012). Examination of the trait facets of the five-factor model in discriminating specific mood and anxiety disorders. *Psychiatry Research*, 199, 131–139.

Reich, J., & Schatzberg, A. (2021). Prevalence, factor structure, and heritability of avoidant personality disorder. *The Journal of Nervous and Mental Disease*, 209(10), 764–772.

Roberts, B. W., & Damian, R. I. (2019). The principles of personality trait development and their relation to psychopathology. In D. B. Samuel, & D. Lynam (Eds.), *Using Basic Personality Research to Inform Personality Pathology* (pp. 153–165). Oxford University Press.

Roberts, B. W., & DelVecchio, W. F. (2000). The rank-order consistency of personality traits from childhood to old age: A quantitative review of longitudinal studies. *Psychological Bulletin*, 126, 3–25.

Roberts, B. W., Kuncel, N. R., Shiner, R., Caspi, A., & Goldberg, L. R. (2007). The power of personality: The comparative validity of personality traits, socio-economic status, and cognitive ability for predicting important life outcomes. *Perspectives on Psychological Science*, 2(4), 313–345.

Roberts, B. W., & Yoon, H. J. (2022). Personality psychology. *Annual Review of Psychology*, 73(1), 489–516.

Robins, R., Fraley, C., & Krueger, R. (2007). *Handbook of Research Methods in Personality Psychology*. Guilford Press.

Rosell, D. R., Futterman, S. E., McMaster, A., & Siever, L. J. (2014). Schizotypal personality disorder: A current review. *Current Psychiatry Reports*, 16, 1–12.

Rothbart, M. K. (2011). *Becoming Who We Are: Temperament and Personality in Development*. Guilford.

Royal College of Psychiatrists. (2020). *Services for People Diagnosable with Personality Disorder*. Royal College of Psychiatrists.

Rush, A. J., Aaronson, S. T., & Demyttenaere, K. (2019). Difficult-to-treat depression: A clinical and research roadmap for when remission is elusive. *Australian & New Zealand Journal of Psychiatry*, 53(2), 109–118.

Rutter, M. (1987). Temperament, personality and personality disorder. *British Journal of Psychiatry*, 150, 443–458.

Rutter, M. (2006). *Genes and Behavior: Nature-Nurture Interplay Explained.* Blackwell.

Rutter, M. (2012). Resilience as a dynamic concept. *Development and Psychopathology, 24*(2), 335–344.

Rutter, M., Beckett, C., Castle, J., Colvert, E., Kreppner, J., Mehta, M., & Sonuga-Barke, E. (2007). Effects of profound early institutional deprivation: An overview of findings from a UK longitudinal study of Romanian adoptees. *European Journal of Developmental Psychology, 4*(3), 332–350.

Rutter, M., Tizard, J., Yule, W., Graham, P., & Whitmore, K. (1976). Isle of Wight studies, 1964–1974. *Psychological Medicine, 6*(2), 313–332.

Salomon, K., & Jin, A. (2020). Diathesis-stress model. In *Encyclopedia of behavioral medicine* (pp. 655–657). Springer International Publishing.

Samuel, D. B., & Widiger, T. A. (2011). Conscientiousness and obsessive-compulsive personality disorder. *Personality Disorders: Theory, Research, and Treatment, 2*(3), 161.

Sauer-Zavala, S., Southward, M. W., Fruhbauerova, M., Semcho, S. A., Stumpp, N. E., Hood, C. O., ... & Cravens, L. (2023). BPD compass: A randomized controlled trial of a short-term, personality-based treatment for borderline personality disorder. *Personality Disorders: Theory, Research, and Treatment, 14*(5), 534.

Sauer-Zavala, S., Wilner, J. G., & Barlow, D. H. (2017). Addressing neuroticism in psychological treatment. *Personality Disorders: Theory, Research, and Treatment, 8*(3), 191.

Savulescu, J., Roache, R., Davies, W., & Loebel, J. P. (Eds.). (2020). *Psychiatry Reborn: Biopsychosocial Psychiatry in Modern Medicine.* Oxford University Press.

Schiepek, G. (2009). Complexity and nonlinear dynamics in psychotherapy. *European Review, 17*(2), 331–356.

Scholte-Stalenhoef, A. N., Pijnenborg, G. H. M., Hasson-Ohayon, I., & Boyette, L. L. (2023). Personality traits in psychotic illness and their clinical correlates: A systematic review. *Schizophrenia Research, 252,* 348–406.

Sellbom, M., Ben-Porath, Y. S., & Bagby, R. M. (2008). Personality and psychopathology: Mapping the MMPI-2 Restructured Clinical (RC) Scales onto the five factor model of personality. *Journal of Personality Disorders, 22*(3), 291–312.

Selten, J. P., Van Der Ven, E., Rutten, B. P., & Cantor-Graae, E. (2013). The social defeat hypothesis of schizophrenia: An update. *Schizophrenia Bulletin, 39*(6), 1180–1186.

Shiner, R. L. (2019). Negative emotionality and neuroticism from childhood through adulthood: A lifespan perspective. In D. McAdams, R. L. Shiner, & J. L. Tackett (Eds.), *Handbook of Personality Development* (pp. 137–152). Guilford Press.

Sigelman, C. K., De George, L., Cunial, K., & Rider, E. A. (2018). *Life Span Human Development* (4th Edition). Cengage.

Simonsen, E., & Paris, J. (2025). The borderline pattern. In B. Bach (Ed.), *ICD-11 Personality Disorders: A Clinician's Guide: Assessment and Treatment* (pp. 69–81). Hogrefe Publishing.

Soeteman, D.,I., Verheul, R., Delimon, J., Meerman, A. M., van den Eijnden, E., Rossum, B. V., Ziegler, U., Thunnissen, M., Busschbach, J. J., & Kim, J. J.

(2010). Cost-effectiveness of psychotherapy for cluster B personality disorders. *British Journal of Psychiatry, 196*, 396–403.

Specht, J., Egloff, B., & Schmukle, S. C. (2011). Stability and change of personality across the life course: The impact of age and major life events on mean-level and rank-order stability of the Big Five. *Journal of Personality and Social Psychology, 101*(4), 862–888.

Spengler, M., Gottschling, J., Spinath, F.M. (2012). Personality in childhood – A longitudinal behavior genetic approach. *Personality and Individual Differences, 53*, 411–416.

Stanton, A. L., Revenson, T. A., & Tennen, H. (2007). Health psychology: Psychological adjustment to chronic disease. *Annual Review of Psychology, 58*(1), 565–592.

Steiger, H., Booji, L., St.-Hilaire, S. A., & Stanton, A. M. (2023). In R. F., Krueger, & P. H. Blaney (Eds.), *Oxford Textbook of Psychopathology* (pp. 424–449). Oxford University Press.

Storebø, O. J., Stoffers-Winterling, J. M., Völlm, B. A., Kongerslev, M. T., Mattivi, J. T., Jørgensen, M. S., ... & Simonsen, E. (2020). Psychological therapies for people with borderline personality disorder. *The Cochrane Database of Systematic Reviews, 5*(5), CD012955.

Sturman, E. D., & Mongrain, M. (2008). The role of personality in defeat: A revised social rank model. *European Journal of Personality, 22*(1), 55–79.

Takahashi, M., Shirayama, Y., Muneoka, K., Suzuki, M., Sato, K., & Hashimoto, K. (2013). Personality traits as risk factors for treatment-resistant depression. *PloS One, 8*(5), e63756.

Tang, A., Crawford, H., Fox, N., & Morales, S. (2020). Shyness trajectories across the first four decades predict mental health outcomes. *Journal of Abnormal Child Psychology, 45*, 1621–1633.

Terracciano, A., McCrae, R. R., & Costa Jr, P. T. (2010). Intra-individual change in personality stability and age. *Journal of research in personality, 44*(1), 31–37.

Tice, D. M., & Baumeister, R. F. (2021). The Psychological Immune System: What needs defending? *Psychological Inquiry, 32*(4), 260–262.

Giesen-Bloo, J., Van Dyck, R., Spinhoven, P., Van Tilburg, W., Dirksen, C., Van Asselt, T., ... & Arntz, A. (2006). Outpatient psychotherapy for borderline personality disorder: Randomized trial of schema-focused therapy vs transference-focused psychotherapy. *Archives of General Psychiatry, 63*(6), 649–658.

Torgersen, S., Lygren, S., Oien, P.A., Skre, I., Onstad, S., Edvardsen, J., et al. (2000). A twin study of personality disorders. *Comprehensive Psychiatry, 41*, 416–425.

True, W. R., Rice, J., Eisen, S. A., Heath, A. C., Goldberg, J., & Lyons, M. J. (1993). A twin study of genetic and environmental contributions to liability for post traumatic stress symptoms. *Archives of General Psychiatry, 50*, 257–264.

Trull, T. J., & Brown, W. C. (2013). Borderline personality disorder: A five-factor model perspective. In T. A. Widiger & P. T. Costa, Jr. (Eds.), *Personality Disorders and the Five-Factor Model of Personality* (3rd ed., pp. 119–132). American Psychological Association.

Trull, T. J., Jahng, S., Tomko, R. L., Wood, P. K., & Sher, K. J. (2010). Revised NESARC personality disorder diagnosis: Gender, prevalence, and comorbidity with substance dependence disorders. *Journal of Personality Disorders, 24,* 412–426.

Trull, T. J., & Sher, K. J. (1994). Relationship between the five-factor model of personality and Axis I disorders in a nonclinical sample. *Journal of Abnormal Psychology, 103*(2), 350–360.

Turiano, N. A., Graham, E. K., Weston, S. J., Booth, T., Harrison, F., James, B. D., ... & Mroczek, D. K. (2020). Is healthy neuroticism associated with longevity? A coordinated integrative data analysis. *Collabra: Psychology, 6*(1), 33.

Tyrer, P., & Mulder, R. (2022). *Personality Disorder: From Evidence to Understanding.* Cambridge University Press.

Tyrer, P., Mulder, R., Kim, Y. R., & Crawford, M. J. (2019). The development of the ICD-11 classification of personality disorders: An amalgam of science, pragmatism, and politics. *Annual Review of Clinical Psychology, 15,* 481–502.

Tyrer, P., & Tyrer, H. (2018). *Nidotherapy: Harmonising the Environment with the Patient* (2nd edition). Cambridge University Press.

van den Berg, S.M., de Moor, M.H.M., Verweij, K.J.H. *et al.* (2016). Meta-analysis of genome-wide association studies for extraversion: Findings from the genetics of personality consortium. *Behaviour Genetics, 46,* 170–182.

Victor, S. E., & Klonsky, E. D. (2016). Validation of a brief version of the difficulties in emotion regulation scale (DERS-18) in five samples. *Journal of Psychopathology and Behavioral Assessment, 38,* 582–589.

Vittersø, J. (2001). Personality traits and subjective well-being: Emotional stability, not extraversion, is probably the important predictor. *Personality and Individual Differences, 31*(6), 903–914.

Vogel, D. L., & Heath, P. J. (2016). Men, masculinities, and help-seeking patterns. In Y. J. Wong & S. R. Wester (Eds.), *APA Handbook of Men and Masculinities* (pp. 685–707). American Psychological Association.

Voineskos, D., Daskalakis, Z. J., & Blumberger, D. M. (2020). Management of treatment-resistant depression: Challenges and strategies. *Neuropsychiatric Disease and Treatment, 16,* 221–234.

Vukasović, T., & Bratko, D. (2015). Heritability of personality: A meta-analysis of behavior genetic studies. *Psychological Bulletin, 141*(4), 769–785.

Walters, S. T., & Rotgers, F. (Eds). (2012). *Treating Substance Abuse: Theory and Technique.* Guilford.

Wampold, B. E. (2015). *The Great Psychotherapy Debate: The Evidence for What Makes Psychotherapy Work .* Routledge.

Wampold, B. E. (2019). *The Basics of Psychotherapy: An Introduction to Theory and Practice.* American Psychological Association.

Watson, D., Clark, L. A., Simms, L. J., & Kotov, R. (2022). Classification and assessment of fear and anxiety in personality and psychopathology. *Neuroscience & Biobehavioral Reviews, 142,* 104878.

Weinberg, I., & Ronningstam, E. (2022). Narcissistic personality disorder: Progress in understanding and treatment. *Focus, 20*(4), 368–377.

Weinbrecht, A., Schulze, L., Boettcher, J., & Renneberg, B. (2016). Avoidant personality disorder: A current review. *Current Psychiatry Reports, 18,* 1–8.

Weiner, I. B. (2003). *Principles of Rorschach Interpretation.* Lawrence Erlbaum.

Weiss, A., & Gartner, M. (2015). Animal personality. In T. A. Widiger (Ed.), *The Oxford Handbook of the Five Factor Model.* Oxford Library of Psychology.

Werner, E. E. (2014). High-risk children in young adulthood: A longitudinal study from birth to 32 years. In R. M. Lerner, & C. M. Ohannessian (Eds.), *Risks and Problem Behaviors in Adolescence* (pp. 76–85). Routledge.

Wetzelaer, P., Lokkerbol, J., Arntz, A., van Asselt, A., & Evers, S. (2016). Cost-effectiveness of psychotherapy for personality disorders. A systematic review on economic evaluation studies. *Tijdschroft voor Psychiatrie, 58,* 717–727.

White, L. K., McDermott, J. M., Degnan, K. A., Henderson, H. A., & Fox, N. A. (2011). Behavioral inhibition and anxiety: The moderating roles of inhibitory control and attention shifting. *Journal of Abnormal Child Psychology, 39,* 735–747.

Whitley, R. (2014). Beyond critique: Rethinking roles for the anthropology of mental health. *Culture, Medicine, and Psychiatry, 38,* 499–511.

Whitman, M. R., Tylicki, J. L., Mascioli, R., Pickle, J., & Ben-Porath, Y. S. (2021). Psychometric properties of the Minnesota Multiphasic Personality Inventory-3 (MMPI-3) in a clinical neuropsychology setting. *Psychological Assessment, 33,* 142–155.

Widiger, T. A. (1998). Four out of five ain't bad. *Archives of General Psychiatry, 55*(10), 865–866.

Widiger, T. A. (Ed.). (2015). *The Oxford Handbook of the Five Factor Model.* Oxford University Press.

Widiger, T. A., & Crego, C. (2019). The Five Factor Model of personality structure: an update. *World Psychiatry, 18*(3), 271.

Widiger, T. A., Lynam, D. R., Miller, J. D., & Oltmanns, T. F. (2012). Measures to assess maladaptive variants of the Five-Factor Model. *Journal of Personality Assessment, 94*(5), 450–455.

Widiger, T. A., & McCabe, G. A. (2020). The Alternative Model of Personality Disorders (AMPD) from the perspective of the five-factor model. *Psychopathology, 53,* 149–156.

Widiger, T. A., & Oltmanns, J. R. (2017). Neuroticism is a fundamental domain of personality with enormous public health implications. *World Psychiatry, 16*(2), 144–145.

Widiger, T., & Smith, M. M. (2025). Personality disorders: Current conceptualizations and challenges. *Annual Review of Clinical Psychology, 21,* 169–192.

Widom, C., Cjaza, C., & Paris, J. (2009). A prospective investigation of borderline personality disorder in abused and neglected children followed up into adulthood. *Journal of Personality Disorders, 23,* 433–446.

Winsper, C. (2018). The aetiology of borderline personality disorder (BPD): Contemporary theories and putative mechanisms. *Current Opinion in Psychology, 21,* 105–110.

Wolke, D., Schreier, A., Zanarini, M. C., & Winsper, C. (2012). Bullied by peers in childhood and borderline personality symptoms at 11 years of age: A prospective study. *Journal of Child Psychology and Psychiatry, 53,* 846–855.

Woo, S. E., Chernyshenko, O. S., Longley, A., Zhang, Z. X., Chiu, C. Y., & Stark, S. E. (2014). Openness to experience: Its lower level structure, measurement, and cross-cultural equivalence. *Journal of Personality Assessment, 96*(1), 29–45.

Wood, J. M., & Lilienfeld, S. O. (1999). The Rorschach Inkblot Test: A case of overstatement? *Assessment, 6,* 341–352.

Wood, J. M., Lilienfeld, S. O., Garb, H. N., & Nezworski, M. T. (2000). The Rorschach test in clinical diagnosis: A critical review, with a backward look at Garfield (1947). *Journal of Clinical Psychology, 56*, 395–430.

World Health Organization. (2018). *International Classification of Diseases* (11th edition). WHO.

World Health Organization. (2021). *Suicide Worldwide in 2019: Global Health Estimates.* WHO.

Yeomans, F., Clarkin, J., & Kernberg, O. (2002). *A Primer for Transference-Focused Psychotherapy for Borderline Personality Disorder.* Jason Aronson.

Zanarini, M. C. (2000). Childhood experiences associated with the development of borderline personality disorder. *Psychiatric Clinics of North America, 23*(1), 89–101.

Zanarini, M. C. (2009). Psychotherapy of borderline personality disorder. *Acta Psychiatrica Scandinavica, 120*, 373–377.

Zanarini, M. C. (2019). *In the Fullness of Time: Recovery from Borderline Personality Disorder.* Oxford University Press.

Zanarini, M. C., Frankenburg, F. R., Glass, I. V., & Fitzmaurice, G. M. (2024). The 24-year course of symptomatic disorders in patients with borderline personality disorder and personality-disordered comparison subjects: Description and prediction of recovery from BPD. *The Journal of Clinical Psychiatry, 85*(3), 24m15370.

Zarei, E., Karami Boldaji, R., Heydari, H., Hossein Khanzadeh, A. A., & Baharloo, G. (2014). Prediction of the five-factor personality traits of students based on adult attachment styles. *Research in Cognitive and Behavioral Sciences, 4*(1), 167–180.

Zhang, L., & Takahashi, Y. (2024). Relationships between obsessive-compulsive disorder and the big five personality traits: A meta-analysis. *Journal of Psychiatric Research.* https://doi.org/10.1016/j.jpsychires.2024.06.033

Zilberman, N., Yadid, G., Efrati, Y., Neumark, Y., & Rassovsky, Y. (2018). Personality profiles of substance and behavioral addictions. *Addictive Behaviors, 82.*

Zilcha-Mano, S. (2021). Toward personalized psychotherapy: The importance of the trait-like/state-like distinction for understanding therapeutic change. *American Psychologist, 76*(3), 516.

Zimmerman, M. (2022). Should the demonstration of improved patient outcome be necessary to overhaul diagnostic approaches? Comment on Bach and Tracy. *Personality Disorders: Theory, Research, and Treatment, 13*, 387–391.

Zimmerman, M., Rothschild, L., & Chelminski, I. (2005). The prevalence of DSM-IV personality disorders in psychiatric outpatients. *American Journal of Psychiatry, 162*, 1911–1918.

Zuckerman, M. (1987). All parents are environmentalists until they have their second child. *Behavioral and Brain Sciences, 10*(1), 42–44.

Index

achievement striving, in
  conscientiousness 7
actions, in openness 7
activity, in extraversion 6
addictive personality 49
adversity 32–5, 38; childhood 57–62;
  environmental 38, 62–3
aesthetics 7
agreeableness xi, xiii, 2, 5, 6, 10, 31,
  79, 81, 84
Allport, G. W. 2
alternative model for personality
  disorders (AMPD) xii, 4, 23, 54–5,
  65
altruism 6
American Psychiatric Association 54
angry hostility 6
anorexia nervosa 49–50
antagonism 5, 10, 56, 65, 79, 81, 84
anti-neurotics 78
antisocial personality disorders (ASPD)
  65–6
anxiety 6, 46–8
Assary, E. 33
assertiveness 6
attachment theory 37–8
avoidant personality disorders (AVPD)
  67, 83–4

Bagby, R. M. 74, 81
Barlow, D. H. 78
Beck, Aaron 73, 92
behavioral inhibition 8
behavior genetics 24–5, 36–7, 63
behavior therapy (BT) 73; see also
  dialectical behavior therapy (DBT)
binge eating disorder 49–50

"bio-bio-bio" theory 41
biological reductionism 64
biopsychosocial (BPS) model viii,
  41–4; "bio-bio-bio" theory 41;
  complex traits 42; emergence 42–4;
  GWAS studies 43; psychological
  immune system 42; reductionism
  42–4; replication crisis 42; scientific
  status xiv
Blaffer Hrdy, Sara 28
borderline personality disorder
  (BPD) xv, 12–13, 55–65; antisocial
  65–6; avoidant 67, 83–4; childhood
  adversity 57–62; Compass 78; as
  complex PTSD 60, 64; diagnosis
  55–6, 83; gene–environment
  interactions 62–4; ICD-11 system
  68–9; life course 57; micro-psychotic
  symptoms 56; narcissistic 66–7;
  obsessive-compulsive 67–8, 84;
  post-traumatic theory 62; treatment
  of 64–5
Bornovalova, M. A. 63
Bowlby, J. 37
bulimia nervosa 49–50

Campbell, Anne 28
candidate genes 43
categorical diagnosis 19, 23, 47, 52–5,
  68–71
childhood adversity 57–62; childhood
  sexual abuse 58–61; emotional
  abuse 59; family dysfunction
  59; neglect 59; physical abuse
  58–9, 61; resilience 59; vulnerable
  temperament 59
childhood sexual abuse (CSA) 58–61